THE PRESCHOOL HANDBOOK

BANK STREET'S COMPLETE PARENT GUIDE

THE PRESCHOOL HANDBOOK

MAKING THE MOST OF YOUR CHILD'S EDUCATION

BY BARBARA BRENNER

PANTHEON BOOKS
NEW YORK

Library of Congress Cataloging-in-Publication Data
Brenner, Barbara.
The preschool handbook : making the most of your child's
education/Barbara Brenner.
p.   cm.
"Bank Street's complete parent guide."
Includes index.
ISBN 0-679-72551-2
1. Education, Preschool—United States.   2. Education, Preschool
—United States—Parent participation.   I. Title.
LB1140.23.B74   1990
372.21—dc20   89-42553

The photographs in this book were taken by Anne-Marie Mott and
are copyright © Bank Street College.

Book Design by Jan Melchior
Manufactured in the United States of America

First Edition

C O N T E N T S

A C K N O W L E D G M E N T S

There is much thanks due on this book—first to my Bank
Street colleagues, particularly Roberta Altman, Nancy
Balaban, Ellen Galinsky, Bob Grainger, Anne Heaney,
Lelita Jaspel, Leah Levinger, Maritza MacDonald, Lo-
renzo Martinez, Anne Mitchell, Kathy Modigliani, Ann-
Marie Mott, Joanne Oppenheim, John Regis, Ann Schafer.

I thank collectively the many parents who talked with
me and responded to my questionnaire. And I owe a great
debt to the teachers, administrators, and other specialists
who gave me the benefit of their expertise—Marilyn Barnwell, Marlene Barron, Camille Centrella, Dr. Joseph Dub-
rosin, Sally Edinger, Susan Feingold, Dr. James Gerson,
Mary Hayes, Cele Mark, Joyce McGinn, Nancy McIndoc,
Janice McLain, Donna Merrick, Jan Miller, Jean Pole-
shuck, John Savidge, Kate Sheeran, Chris Snyder, Sharon
Willow, Donna Woehrle.

Special thanks go to Tom Engelhardt, my editor at Pantheon, whose deep commitment to the project helped shape
both the concept and the book itself; to Bill Hooks and

Jim Levine, my in-house editorial support; and to Margaret Peet, who helped transform my many drafts and cut-paper puzzles into a finished manuscript.

Last, but certainly not least, my thanks and gratitude go to my consultant, Alison Pepper, Early Childhood Consultant to the Bureau of Day Care of the City of New York and former preschool director. Alison's intelligence, her special experience, and her insights illumine every page.

INTRODUCTION

If you're a parent and have been thinking about some form of preschool for your youngster, more than likely you're finding yourself slogging through a welter of unfamiliar terms and confusing concepts. Even if you know what preschool is and have sorted out the differences between day care, nursery school, public pre-K, and other types of preschools, finding the one that suits your youngster may not be easy. You may have resigned yourself to the idea that helping your youngster choose a college someday is going to be a complex and frustrating task. It comes as something of a shock to discover that searching out a quality preschool program for a three-year-old can have some of the same complexities.

In fact, the two searches are in some ways similar. At both stages you're looking for a good match between youngster, parent, and school—something that squares with both the young person's individual personality and capabilities and your own particular set of standards and requirements (financial, geographic, and whatever other conditions you choose to put into the equation). But there's where the analogy breaks down. Whereas you can find detailed information on any college or university in the United States (or the world, for that matter), there is very little such information available for preschools, except from the schools themselves. In spite of the widely held conviction that preschool is a vital time in a child's life, the majority of programs and settings for three-, four-, and five-year-olds remain pretty much without enforceable standards and without the kinds of licensing that other educational settings are required to have. What this means, for most parents, is that you'll have to search out a good preschool. Depending on what your child is like, where you live, how much you can spend, and what kind of setting you need, you may have many choices or too few.

This is a book about good preschool—what it is, how to find it, and what you as a parent can do to make it as good as it can be. But, to begin with, it may be useful to walk the terrain—to get a sense of the big picture—of what we think is important, the issues we're going to highlight, and how you can best use this book.

PRESCHOOL: THE BIG PICTURE

Thinking about preschool can evoke some very personal feelings for parents. There's always plenty of guilt, especially in single-parent households or where both parents are working. Working or not, you may be a little hesitant about sending your child to preschool. Indeed, it's a big step, allowing your young one to be somewhere else for a major part of the day, in the care of strangers. Some parents may question whether preschool isn't another antifamily invention, born of the feminist movement and the double work force.

It may be both reassuring and informative here to take

a quick look backward at where the idea of preschool came from and how long it's been going on.

A SHORT HISTORY OF PRESCHOOL

In reality, what happens in today's nursery schools and other preschool settings has its roots in ideas that were formulated hundreds of years ago, not only in the United States but in Germany, Italy, England, and other European countries. Indeed, today's preschool in Urbana, Illinois, or the child care center in Poughkeepsie, New York, can claim kinship with the ''dame schools'' that were operating in Boston, Massachusetts, as early as the 1600s. These academic classes for young children were often run by widows in their own homes. The women were paid by parents to teach their three-, four-, and five-year-olds to read and memorize passages from the Bible. There was a real passion for education among the Puritans, and it's interesting to note that it was education for use. The Puritans, quite simply, wanted their children to read early so that they could read the Good Book, which was the cornerstone of daily life in New England. They also felt strongly that to know how to read was to be able to live by the laws of the colonies. This idea of ''learning real-life skills'' as opposed to learning isolated from life may be the contribution of the Puritans to present-day preschool thought.

Johann Pestalozzi was probably the father of a coherent philosophy of early childhood education. A Swiss born in 1746, Pestalozzi was neither a scholar nor particularly well educated. What he did have was a great feeling for children and the kind of nurture they needed. He sensed, for example, that public education had to ''take into consideration the circumstances of family life.'' He believed that schools for young children should have the warmth and caring atmosphere that parents would give at home. He felt that teachers should be somewhat like surrogate parents. He believed that it was useful for children to teach one another as well as to have a teacher. And he didn't think teachers should use a "wordy method of teaching" with young children. All of these were revolutionary ideas in the middle of the eighteenth century, but they found their way into good preschool education and remained there.

Friedrich Froebel, who was born in 1782 in Germany, studied Pestalozzi's work. Froebel is responsible for the concept of kindergarten. But perhaps Froebel's bigger contribution is the fact that he gave us a new concept of childhood. Before Froebel, children were generally regarded as imperfectly formed or miniature adults. Froebel contributed the novel notion that childhood was not just a time of preparing for adulthood but a separate learning and growing time that had value in itself. In his model of preschool, his "child's garden," children played, as a part of their learning.

There was one more piece to Froebel's model that has modern-day resonance. Froebel's kindergarten introduced the idea that home and school should to some extent physically merge. In Froebel's kindergarten, part of the day was in the home, where teachers spent time with children and their mothers, sharing aspects of the child's education. This partnership between parents and teachers is a strong component of most good preschool programs today, and a central theme of this book.

Robert Owen's Infant School movement started in England around the beginning of the nineteenth century. Owen, whose family owned a cotton mill, was concerned about the mill workers' children, whom he saw growing up in poverty and ignorance. In a way you might consider Owen's experiment the first corporate preschool. Owen was an enlightened employer who instituted a child care education center for his workers.

Actually, Owen's educational agenda was broader than just taking care of his own workers' families. He wanted to service all poor children and felt that they could be taught better in his school than at home or in the then-current primary schools. Owen's preschool introduced some new and daring ideas. One was that in addition to teaching young children specific concepts and allowing them time to play and be creative, a school should have some responsibility for building a child's character. The other was that everyone, including children, had the right to happiness and that early education should do its part in providing it. Lastly, he believed passionately that the childhood years were important in people's lives.

The Owen Infant Schools were widely copied in the United States, especially after Owen came to this country and settled in New Harmony, Indiana. Bronson Alcott, the father of Louisa May, founded and for some years ran an Owen school.

The original Owen schools were designed for students three to ten years old. But Owen's ideas captured the imagination of forward-looking parents of younger children as well. Soon you could find toddlers as young as eighteen months old in the activity-oriented Owen settings. And although many of the first Owen schools followed his precept of special education for the needy, later Owen preschools tended to be for the affluent.

Maria Montessori, an Italian doctor, came to her theories about teaching young children through her work with mentally retarded youngsters. Studying and teaching these children, most of whom were from deprived backgrounds, she came to certain conclusions about all children. Montessori felt that children "unfold" regardless of environment, given the proper stimulation at the proper time. She saw all young children as going through certain stages of development, each geared to certain types of learning. Therefore, she designed special learning materials to mesh with these stages and then suggested that the teacher and the older children in a school act as mentors in shaping the younger child's innate capabilities. In a sense, it was Maria Montessori who introduced the concept of specially designed materials and of ''self-connecting'' toys. These ideas are utilized in many good preschool programs and are guiding principles in Montessori schools.

Bringing nature into the nursery is a time-honored way of teaching science.

PRESCHOOLS IN THE TWENTIETH CENTURY

The first ''nursery school'' was established in England by Rachel and Margaret MacMillan in 1911. Although it was called a nursery school, a term that has different connotations today, it was actually more like our modern day care center. Children stayed from early morning until 5:30 in the evening or even later. They were fed and taught how to do basic health routines. But the MacMillans felt that physical care, while important, was only part of the necessities for children. Education was the second piece of the picture. In MacMillan schools the children received formal lessons in the three Rs by the age of five. Animals were kept in the nursery, and children of all ages had responsibilities for feeding and caring for them. Nature was part of the classroom in the MacMillan nursery, as was physical movement and music and art. The MacMillan nursery school was widely emulated and is still considered a textbook model to study.

There are many other educators besides these five who actually founded preschools or whose ideas are embedded in present early childhood programs. It's interesting in view of the present debate in some quarters over out-of-home care and education to see what a venerable history the idea has. However, there's one thing that should be noted about these early efforts. Most of them were designed to help poor and disadvantaged children learn. Yet all of them later filtered up to the middle class, where they largely remained for a long time.

In 1916 Lucy Sprague Mitchell founded the Bureau for Educational Experiments, which was to become the Bank Street School for Children. Mitchell gathered around her experts in all phases of child development—pediatricians, psychologists, educators, researchers—to take one of the first holistic looks at young children. The Bureau was one among a number of experiments in early childhood education that was to introduce the idea of looking at childhood in a more complete way and developing an early childhood program that came out of scientific study. As a body of research on child development grew and results were better able to be tabulated, preschools using this model proliferated in various parts of the United States as well as in other countries.

PRESCHOOL AND THE GREAT DEPRESSION

When the Great Depression came, the focus of these programs returned to some of the preschool movement's original precepts, that is, to help the needy. Preschool day care programs in public schools began to serve the needs of working-class families through the WPA (Works Progress Administration) and other subsidized programs. Interestingly these programs satisfied another agenda as well; they employed thousands of out-of-work teachers. World War II saw the rise of yet another version of preschool in the day care for preschoolers provided to women factory workers under the Lanham Act.

During the postwar years, as a result of new and pioneering studies by adherents of many different educational philosophies, it became increasingly clear that early childhood was an important, maybe even a crucial time in the lives of children. If this was so, then by whatever measurements one used, a large segment of the young population was being seriously shortchanged. Differences were especially marked between very poor youngsters and the middle-class children who were being provided with a rich environment of language and experiences.

At the same time that scientific tests were validating what Owen, Montessori, and others had found, important changes in family patterns were taking place. Women were again becoming a major part of the labor force, and there were significantly more single-parent families. These new patterns, coupled with a new understanding of how young children develop, changed the face of preschool education.

THE ESTABLISHMENT OF HEAD START

The biggest step was the establishment in 1964 of Operation Head Start, a federally funded preschool program designed to meet the needs of working-class families caught in a cycle of poverty and disadvantage. The advent of Head Start meant that poor children for the first time had programs that fostered self-worth, independence, motivation, initiative, and the ability to learn and achieve. Head Start revitalized the Froebelian kindergarten idea of parent participation and training; parent involvement was and is a "given" of all Head Start programs.

Head Start (which Bank Street College helped design) became a model for many other preschool programs. Meanwhile the variety of school types in the preschool marketplace grew. Soon there were preschools run by parents, preschools in the workplace, state-subsidized centers, and college- and university-based programs, as well as chains of commercial preschools that had emerged to satisfy the growing need for preschool.

PRESCHOOL TODAY

Today Friedrich Froebel's ideas live on in the concept of kindergarten in the public schools. Some of the MacMillans' ideas can be seen in modern day care settings. Montessori's theories about innate behaviors influenced later theorists and founded a nationwide Montessori movement. Whether or not these exact models still exist, the important thing is that preschool is no Johnny-come-lately in the annals of child rearing.

However, there were times, historically, when the spotlight seemed to be off early childhood programs. A good example is that thirty years ago *preschool* wasn't even a word in common usage. Only about 15 percent of four-year-olds attended nursery school or some other form of preschool, and these were generally the children of affluent families. If you lived in a metropolis and were sufficiently needy, you might have sent your youngster to one of the few government-subsidized day care centers that were available at that time. If you were a working mother, you had a housekeeper or a neighbor or relative who took care of your child. If you did none of the above (which would have put you in the majority), your child simply stayed home until the age of five, played in the neighborhood, and then went off to kindergarten. Kindergarten itself was an option that was often skipped.

But the preschool idea seems to have phoenixlike staying power. From 1981 to 1986 the number of three-to-five-year-olds in preschool jumped 25 percent. In the year 1989 there will be between 6 and 7 million children going to preschool, according to the latest projections of the National Center for Education Statistics. These figures don't include the thousands of youngsters who will be on a list and waiting to get in, or whose parents will be shopping for a preschool, or wondering whether they should send their boy or girl this year or wait until next.

Today on any weekday morning, in any city, suburb, or exurb, you can see a mass movement of young children of various ages. You see them in cars, on buses, and on foot, accompanied by Mom, Dad, sister or brother, carpool neighbor, or caregiver. Some of them cart lunch boxes. Others cradle a favorite stuffed cat or teddy in their arms. A few clutch a piece of beloved blanket or an item for show-and-tell. You can be fairly certain that the majority of these young citizens are headed for some form of preschool.

WHO'S GOING TO PRESCHOOL?

There are many reasons for this newest incarnation of preschool. The single most powerful one is that there are now more than 18 million children under the age of five in the United States, and 57 percent of the mothers of these young children are working. Nineteen percent of the under-fives live in single-parent families headed by females. These new patterns of family life drive the subject of preschool more than any others that we will be talking about in this book.

But it would be a mistake to assume that it's only single parents and double working families who are filling up the preschools, just as it would be wrong to imply that young children of today are going to preschool only because their families are separated or because their mothers are working. Preschool seems to be attracting families from all walks of life. In fact, according to a May 1988 article in *Principal* magazine, between 1975 and 1984 the greatest attendance growth was in private preschools serving white, high-income children whose mothers weren't working. Preschool education is seen as a priority among both working and nonworking families and among parents of all socioeconomic groups. Even new parents are already think ing about preschool for their youngsters, wondering if it's a good idea, and when would be the optimum time to start.

The issue of child care generally—and preschool specifically—is one of the most talked-about issues in America today. Both political parties in the most recent presidential election put it in their platforms, and legislators from every state are beginning to understand that the country's future as well as their own political fortunes may depend on who cares for and educates our youngest citizens and how good a job is done.

12

In this sense, parents and legislators may now, for the first time, be on the same wavelength. Both groups appreciate that preschool is only one piece of a larger child care issue. They also recognize that preschool is where child care and education most clearly overlap. However, the expanded awareness on the part of business and government has certainly not yet begun to translate into quality preschool settings for everyone all across the country. That's the reason you will find in this book not only what is available in the here and now but some of the strategies other people have tried or that you can try to make good preschool a reality for your three-to-five-year-old.

To sum up, certainly it is clear that early childhood is the place where children can have some of their most significant learning experiences. This being the case, we have pulled together what we think it's important for parents to know about preschool, including how you go about finding one and, once having found the quality setting, what you, working in partnership with both child and teacher, can do to follow through.

How to Use This Book

Because there are so many young children in various kinds of child care settings, some educators are beginning to think of all children from six months on as preschoolers. A more useful breakdown, and one we will use throughout the book, is to consider preschoolers youngsters from about three to five—that is, from somewhere after toddlerhood to before kindergarten. However, if you're a parent of a child under three or one who's pushing six, you may still be interested in preschool, and you may still find that many of the issues discussed here apply to you. For example, if you're thinking about preschool for the future, or if your child missed kindergarten because of a birth-date cut-off, you should find out more about preschool. If your youngster is presently in a toddler care program you like, you may discover that a program suitable for a toddler may not necessarily be the one you want for your preschooler, or you may change your ideas about what you like after reading chapters 2 and 3.

If your child is already in or at the edge of entry into kindergarten, you're beyond the scope of this book. You may want to go to *The Elementary School Handbook* by Joanne Oppenheim (Pantheon), which is the companion to this volume and which explores how to make elementary school work.

Chapter 2 is designed to be a user-friendly resource on the forms of preschool available today, including traditional half-day nursery programs and full-time preschool-child care / day care—private, public, corporate, and subsidized. It will help you sort out some of the big differences among these settings and suggest ways for you to look at, evaluate, and make your choice among the programs. Given the fact that you're not going to find a preschool setting that's perfect in every respect, chapter 3 will tell you what's most important and what you can afford to overlook. It will also offer a firsthand look inside several actual preschools so that on a more personal level you can read about the sorts of experiences of other parents and children that can inform your choice. Chapter 4 will give you a picture of a typical preschool day.

But finding a good preschool for your youngster is only half the story. The other half is making preschool work. *The Preschool Handbook* is based on the conviction that a good preschool experience is founded on a three-way partnership between you, your child, and the teacher. Chapters 5 through 9 will help you negotiate this sometimes rocky terrain, and we'll discuss some of the issues that are likely to surface. You'll find such subjects as separation, timing, teacher conferences, and supporting preschool at home. All of them are looked at from the perspective of working as cooperatively as possible with the preschool teacher in the interests of your child. You'll also find answers to some special questions you may have—on issues such as testing, stress, and how preschool links with kindergarten.

You may want to read these chapters once through as background before your child starts preschool. Then you may want to go back and read specific chapters when an issue arises. You may also want to share some of the material with your child's teacher and with other parents.

Finally, chapter 10 will help you help your child make a smooth transition from preschool to kindergarten and will give you some perspectives on the future of preschool in this country.

THE PRESCHOOL MARKETPLACE

—

A WORKING DEFINITION OF PRESCHOOL

In spite of the fact that preschool is rapidly becoming almost a given of early childhood, there's a lot of confusion about exactly what it is. What does the word *preschool* mean? What ages does it cover? How does it differ from other forms of child care, or doesn't it? Are there different kinds of preschool? What are the differences?

To begin with, the name itself is misleading, implying as it does a sort of mini or first school that provides aca-

16

demic preparation for regular school. "We're not *pre*-anything," says Marlene Barron, who directs a Montessori preschool in New York City. Barron went on to point out that while the benefits of preschool certainly carry over into regular school, its name tends to make parents focus on possible future advantages, which can distort preschool's very real value as a rich experience in and of itself.

So, if it isn't school, what is it? Briefly, preschool can be any one of a number of professional early childhood settings where a child plays and learns, has a variety of experiences, and meets other children in a friendly, homey atmosphere. Preschool can be set in a church, a storefront, a school building. It can be held in a converted house, a building attached to a factory, or on a college campus. A good preschool setting is always equipped with interesting toys, plenty of books and games, and outdoor space of some kind where a child can run around. It has a professionally run *program,* administered by professionally trained, caring adults with whom the child can develop close ties and who treat him or her with respect and affection.

Can a child care or day care center be preschool? Yes. Is nursery school preschool? Again, yes. You'll find the terms *preschool, child care center,* and *nursery school* used here pretty interchangeably. Because, in fact, preschool education can be found in a variety of settings. We'll also be using the word *caregiver* sometimes and *teacher* other times to indicate the fact that in the preschool age group they are often one and the same. But not always.

Types of Preschool

As we've already suggested, preschool comes in many different forms and is called by different names. Some of the name differences aren't important; it's just that you can

17

sometimes find a preschool more readily in the Yellow Pages if you know that it may be listed separately under "Nursery Schools," "Child Care Centers," or "Pre-Kindergarten Schools," or that it may be hidden within a larger private or public school listing.

Preschool also comes in different sizes; there are programs set up for a few youngsters and for a few hundred. There are religious preschools and secular ones, settings that emphasize academics, others that focus on social development, and some that do both. It's important to know that unlike elementary schools, which differ somewhat from district to district but have generally similar curricula, preschools present a wide variety of both physical settings and educational programs.

Even their schedules differ from one another. You can choose to send a child to preschool for part of every day, for a full five-day week, or for part of the day part of the week. Some settings give a child lunch or dinner or both meals. Others provide only a snack. Still others require that a youngster bring his or her own lunch.

Sometimes the name of a preschool can give you a clue as to the hours, if not to the rest of the program. For example, if it's called *day care,* you know that it is open from early in the morning until late in the evening (sometimes as late as eight o'clock). *Nursery school* generally means a half-day program (but not always). More children from three to five attend half-day programs than full-day programs.

Keeping in mind that the name itself doesn't tell you anything about quality, here is a rundown of some of the broad generic types of preschool education that are available in today's market. Chapter 3 will give you a more detailed picture of them.

One common form of preschool is attached to or part of

an *independent,* or *private school.* The Bank Street Children's School is one example of this configuration. Montessori schools are another, and there are many others all over the country. In this private school model the preschool is often called the *lower school.* Here three-, four-, and five-year-olds (sometimes sixes) play and learn in rooms separate from the older children and with teachers who usually have special training in early childhood education. The educational program of private preschools that have elementary schools attached is consistent with the philosophy of the rest of the school. In fact, preschoolers in these kinds of settings sometimes continue up the grades in the same school. Others go on to public school or to other private schools.

Private preschools don't have one standard set of hours. The Lower School of the Bank Street Children's School is open for the same number of hours as the rest of the school. For parents who work, there's an optional afterschool program. Private preschools are the most expensive form of preschool, and if they have a good reputation, they're often hard to get into.

Day care center (often called *child care center*) usually means that a full day of care is available—hence the name. The day may begin as early as 8:00 A.M. or even earlier. It may go to 7:00 P.M. or even later. A day care center or child care center can accommodate parents who have to go to work early and come home late. In a day care–type preschool program, your youngster will probably get a hot lunch and often will be provided with breakfast and/or supper. Day care centers are usually open twelve months a year, and children can be enrolled at any time during the year. Age ranges in day care centers vary. Some centers only take children above two years old. Others have infants and toddlers in the same setting, but in a different room or rooms. (In most large cities there are special licensing requirements for taking infants and toddlers.) In most states day care centers that enroll five or more children for more than three hours a day must meet very specific state and/or city requirements, such as a set minimum ratio of teachers to children. This is protection for you as a parent in terms of health and safety, but it doesn't guarantee a quality program in every respect.

Day care and child care centers can be partly or wholly subsidized by government agencies, by private foundations, or by corporations. They can be individually or corporately owned, run for profit, or administered as nonprofit parent cooperatives. They can be part of a chain of centers, like the Kindercare chain. Comparing a large day care/child care center with a privately owned suburban preschool is like comparing a university with a small private college. One thing you should know: in a recent study (the National Day Care Study) small group size was found to be one indicator of quality in preschool. Preschoolers in smaller group settings tended to get more out of it than youngsters in larger centers, even when the ratio of teachers to children was the same.

Nursery schools and *play schools* have been in existence for a long time. Often more flexible than other forms of preschool, they usually have a program of a half day. In a setting like this you can often design your child's schedule. A youngster can go for about three hours, from two to five days a week. Here you may pay based on how often your child attends.

Because some children go to nursery school for only a few hours a week, there may be less continuity in a nursery school preschool than in a full-time child care setting. However, this doesn't necessarily mean that there is less value in preschool for only a few hours a week or an hour or two a day. A nursery school–type setting can be great for a three-year-old who's not ready to separate from his parents for longer periods of time. It can serve as a welcome break in routine for a youngster who is at home and needs a taste of independence and sociability. Possibly the best thing about the nursery school model of preschool is that it is often informal. Mom or Dad can stay around and help or leave and come back. Jenny can choose to go or to stay home. In other words, it's not a ''must,'' it's a pleasant option. If a child enjoys it, and a parent wants or needs that private time, a nursery or play school may fill the preschool bill, either before all-day preschool or before kindergarten.

Nursery schools, play schools, and other private half-day preschools are listed in the phone book under those headings or under identifying names, such as Wee Learners or Building Blocks for Kids. They're harder to identify in many communities because they don't have the same licensing requirements as day care and private preschools, so agencies may not have complete records on them. Nursery and play schools may voluntarily register for certification, but they don't have to in most states. As a result, it's possible that the director will have a degree in education but the staff may not. In a nursery school you may have the benefit of small group size but not the other element that is crucial—trained professionals and a thoroughly professional program.

Head Start is the oldest free federally funded preschool program for three-to-five-year-olds. It operates in all fifty states. It is set up to provide a comprehensive child development program, including health, nutrition, education, and social services, and is designed primarily for children from low-income families who are ''at risk'' educationally because of poverty or other disadvantage. Head Start pro-

21

grams are available for part of the day or all day and are administered by a variety of public agencies, depending on the state. They are not always called by this name, but can be identified pretty readily in each community through social agencies.

Some Head Start programs are held in the public school to which a youngster will be going later on. This is a decided advantage in terms of a youngster's adjustment. In rural areas, some Head Start programs are home-based. Workers come to the house and work with parent and child. One powerful component of Head Start is its comprehensive parent-support program. Ten percent of Head Start enrollment is earmarked for physically or emotionally handicapped youngsters, regardless of parent income.

School-Connected Pre-Kindergarten (Pre-K) programs are a relatively new form of preschool. So far twenty-eight states have some form of pre-K funding in place and have either initiated or are expanding experimental programs at the preschool level. They are called by different names in different states; New York City's experiment is called Project Giant Step. More than half of all state-funded pre-K programs are for four-year-olds, and two-thirds of them limit enrollment to low-income, handicapped, and in some cases non-English-speaking youngsters.

Pre-K programs may be funded and administered by the school district or by a private educational contractor with local subsidies. If they're administered by the school district, they may have, in addition to a basic program, whatever other services the public school system provides. In other words, if the school system offers health and social services, parent involvement, and a developmental program, the pre-K program will often have those components too.

So far, most of the new pre-K programs are on a half-day schedule or follow the public school hours. However, because many of the eligible youngsters come from families that work, there is pressure to extend pre-K to a full day. Some educators are in favor of a full day, others oppose it. How this debate is resolved may be very important to you. As your youngster approaches the age when you're going to be making choices, you'll want to keep in touch with developments in your community.

Pre-K programs are not standard; a study in 1987 by Fern Marx, Michelle Seligson, and the Bank Street College of Education (the Public School Early Childhood Study) tells how much was being done by each state at that time. But since the pre-K scene is changing so rapidly, you're probably better off simply calling your own school district when you're ready. If you want to get a feel for how a projected pre-K program in your area will shape up, you may want to take a look at the rest of your district's public schools. This may provide you with some insights as to what the school system thinks about children and learning.

To sum up, here is a general view of how much preschool education is available at this time:

According to the National Association of Young Children and other sources, there are about 39,000 licensed child care centers in existence right now. Statistics on nursery and private schools are hard to come by, but we do know that many more three- and four-year-olds go to private preschools than to public ones. More than 150 companies offer on-site care, and about 3,000 offer subsidized care, financial assistance, or child care referral. Head Start, the oldest federally funded preschool program, services more than 400,000 children, mostly ages three and four, and doesn't begin to take care of the number of children eligible for the program. Kindercare, the largest of the private providers of child care to children from infancy through preschool, has more than 1,100 centers in 40 states. Among the many pre-K and preschool programs funded and/or administered by public agencies, the largest are in Texas, California, New York, Illinois, South Carolina, Massachusetts, and Michigan.

The hardest thing for a parent to come to terms with is the reality that where you live may determine the kind of preschool your child can have. A parent in California may be able to choose from columns A to Z, while a family in rural Pennsylvania may have limited options in terms of preschool. Geography is definitely a part of the equation, as is the fact that while in large cities you have more choices as to the kind of preschools available, you may also have to deal with longer waiting lists.

WHY PRESCHOOL?

Preschool from a parent's perspective is all about choices. Your choice may be not only which preschool, but even if preschool is what you want. Unlike later schooling, pre-kindergarten education is not mandatory—at least not yet. And for many parents it is expensive. You can be influenced by local availability of quality settings and the fact that some educators say that good preschool is good for young children. But in the last analysis it's up to you. You have to look at your child, at the rest of your family, and at your life.

Let's examine some of the reasons why you as a parent may be thinking about preschool for your boy or girl:

You are the mother or father of a three-, four-, or five-year-old and you're either going back to work or to school or have recently started working. Perhaps you're recently divorced or separated. Or maybe you're resuming a professional career after taking time off to be with your youngster. You need for your child to be cared for on a regular basis. What you're after is good care, but you want something above and beyond a caring person who will push your children on the swings in the playground and give them lunch. In other words, you want quality care *plus*.

If you fit this profile, you're probably typical of a great number of today's parents of young children, and you have probably assessed your situation correctly. For working parents, good preschool can indeed be care plus. However, there are some pretty good reasons for a child from three to five to go to preschool that go beyond care plus.

A working parent whose child is presently being cared for at home may think it's time for a change. My friend Vicki expressed it this way: "The caregiver was very loving and devoted. But I didn't think Jeff was getting enough activity and stimulation being with her at home. She hardly ever took him out to play. And she was always talking to him about being 'good,' which in her vocabulary meant staying clean and not doing very much of anything. I just thought he was ready to be in a more lively environment, with people who were more in touch with the needs of children." The desire for a different kind of care is another reason why parents may look to preschool.

A nonworking parent may be motivated by pretty much the same basic urge to provide something that home can't altogether supply. One father confided, in wonderment, "Shana is like a little sponge. She soaks up everything we tell her. I think she needs more in her day than we can possibly supply." This father is obviously looking at preschool as an add-on to his daughter's home environment.

Another reason for preschool may surface if you're a family that lives in a place where your three-, four-, or five-year-old has few chances to meet other children. On the rare occasions when she does connect with other kids, you may notice that she may not know how to act with them. Or she may seem lonely and in need of friends. Or she may seem too dependent on Mom or Dad for entertainment. If you're thinking, *How can I get my child together with some youngsters her own age?* the social aspects of preschool could be as important to you as any of the others.

Parents generally know their child's strengths. Some children are naturally quiet, others are naturally active and even boisterous. One advantage of a good preschool program is that a professional can often bring the quiet child out of her shell and take the rambunctious one down a decibel level or two. The shy child, the nonverbal youngster, the physically less coordinated child—all can benefit from good preschool experience. Quality preschool can help a child develop in a more rounded way. It can foster independence and help children become more organized.

There's one other important reason for you to seek out a preschool. If you are alone, if you have to work and can't afford care for your child at home, if you don't have time to spend with your youngster, or if you are burdened by family problems, you should look into preschool. Families that have heavy financial and/or other problems that affect their children and put them at risk may be eligible for a number of preschool programs that are designed specifically to help them. These programs have been shown to work. The best example is the study of the long-term effects of three different quality preschool programs for disadvantaged children done in 1986 by three prominent educators, Lawrence Schweinhart, David Weikart, and Mary B. Larner. They found that in all three programs children's IQ scores rose significantly and that many of the children's social adjustments to later adolescence were significantly better than those of youngsters from similar backgrounds who had not had the benefit of these preschool programs.

If a child is "at risk" educationally, either because of poverty, a language barrier, or multiple family problems, preschool can be one way to give such a youngster a better start. However, middle-class parents should keep in mind that the dramatic results that showed up in this study can't be inferred for other groups of children in other types of quality preschool programs.

Which leads to the next point, and one of the themes we'll be developing later in the book. There are a few things that preschool can't and shouldn't be expected to deliver. Some mothers and fathers see preschool mainly as a place for a youngster to get a jump start up the competitive ladder. They choose a preschool for its promise to teach computer skills or the track record of its five-year-old alumni in getting into the most prestigious private elementary schools or in skipping kindergarten. These are not good reasons to send a child to preschool, and indeed they may have serious negative consequences for everyone in the family. One danger in this approach to preschool is that it can prevent a youngster from getting the most out of what preschool has to offer. This is not to say that there aren't learning perks inherent in preschool. But there are many other benefits of a good preschool that far outweigh the purely academic, even though they may be less readily measurable.

On balance, preschool can be a milestone in the life of a young child. For most youngsters, it is their first step on the education trail—their introduction to teachers, to classroom routines, to group play, and to more organized learning. Because it's a first in so many ways, children take away from preschool powerful impressions that color their future lives, both in and out of school.

Having said all this, it is still your choice. Nowhere is it written that a child must go to preschool or that the youngster who doesn't go is necessarily deprived. Educator Edward Zigler says flatly, "There is little if anything to be gained by exposing middle-class children to early education." Statistics proving that preschool makes all kids better or smarter or more sociable just don't exist, probably because many of the things children get from quality preschool—social and emotional benefits, independence, creative thinking skills—are not easily measured with standard tests. You as a parent know better than anyone how your child is growing and developing. You can evaluate your needs, the child's needs, and the needs of the whole family. One parent I know said, "I didn't send my first child to preschool and I'm not going to send my second. I was looking forward to staying home with my children until they're ready for kindergarten, and that's what I'm going to do. My husband and I share the care, so between us we'll take on the job." And she added that she was going to personally fight it if her school district mandated public pre-K.

You know if your youngster is curious and lively, if he's having interesting and enriching concrete experiences, and whether he's connecting with books and toys as well as with other children and adults. If all of this is in place, you may decide that preschool is not that important in your family's life.

There's one more thing you should feel easy about. Other things being equal, it is legitimate to beg off on preschool on financial grounds. You may feel that three thousand dollars a year or more for private preschool is simply not a priority for your family, in view of college down the road or mortgage payments or other children's needs. You may elect to enrich your youngster in other ways, such as music lessons or a tumbling class at the Y or family day trips to the zoo or a museum. You can get books at the library. And storytime regularly on a loved one's lap is still one of the nicest ways to enrich a child. Edward Zigler is convinced that because parents and kids share a common life and frame of reference, what they talk about together has great personal meaning. In other words, events and ideas may be conveyed better at home than in other settings—even preschool. No parent should feel guilty for choosing this kind of alternative agenda. But you'll want to look at the summary checklist at the end of this chapter anyway, just in case next year you feel differently.

THE PRESCHOOL PROGRAM

At the heart of every preschool is the program. The program is reflected in the equipment and toys at the center, in the ways in which the caregivers/teachers and children interact, even in the physical space and design of the setting. The program mirrors the philosophy of the center or nursery school; in fact, in a very real sense, it *is* the preschool.

One of the first things you'll notice in a good preschool setting is that the elements of the program have a certain casualness and informality. There may appear to be no plan to the day or the morning. But, in fact, behind this seeming lack of structure are a number of principles and practices that have been carefully designed and refined to mesh with the special learning styles of children from three to five.

THE MAGIC YEARS

It's no accident that so many educators have focused on this particular band of childhood. Of all the ages and stages that children go through, no time seems to have more potential for learning than these early years. Child specialist Selma Fraiberg referred to them as "the magic years" in her classic book of that title. And magic they are. No parent or teacher can fail to be awed by the dazzling acquisition of language, of motor development and coordination, of intuitive and logical learning that can occur in youngsters from week to week, even day to day during the time after they begin to talk and to communicate thoughts and before they start formal academic learning. Barbara Biber, whose specialty is learning and young children, talks about the high degree of "plasticity" of this time in a child's life. Burton White, another early childhood specialist, feels that early childhood is the prime time to shape a child's development in optimum ways. Biber, White, and other educators and psychologists have all done research showing that the preschool years have a special role to play in growth and development. Many of the patterns for learning and growth, for later school and social success, are laid down in the preschool years. That's a powerful reason for a well-thought-out preschool program that takes full advantage of the magic years.

The big difference between a preschool program and later school curricula lies in the way young children learn. The Swiss psychologist Jean Piaget was probably one of the greatest influences on our understanding of this process. He was able to show that young children learn not so much through being "taught" as by playing and experimenting with actual objects and by having concrete experiences. For example, a child learns the concept of "round" not by having someone tell her what round is or what it looks like but by holding and touching, playing and comparing, drawing and cutting round shapes. Piaget showed that young children "think by doing," that spoken language follows thought and activity rather than being separate from it. All these processes have a general developmental timetable. This notion of encouraging learning that is appropriate to the child's age and stage of development is now standard in quality nursery school/preschool programs. Good preschool programs reflect Piagetian principles in the rich variety of materials they make available to children, in their encouragement of dramatic and other kinds of play, and in the "hands-on" activities that give children the opportunity to explore the world around them in many ways.

ACADEMIC PROGRAMS

What about preschool programs that claim to do more than give a child room to play and have concrete social and learning experiences? If it were just a matter of more being better, then the answer would be simple. The best program would be the one that offered a potpourri of math, science, computer techniques, and foreign languages as well as tennis and violin lessons. Preschool programs could be designed that would move second grade down to kindergarten, fourth grade to second, and so on. More things could simply be packed in between the ages of three and five. Indeed, this is precisely the concept of some preschool programs. There's a preschool in Houston, Texas, whose founder boasts that the school is teaching three-year-olds French and computer science. Some of today's preschools claim to teach reading and writing, while others emphasize worksheets for three-year-olds that are similar to what six-year-olds get in public school.

Is an intensely academic, highly structured, "more is better" program a good one? Usually not. Although there may be a few children who seem to thrive in academically oriented programs, the consensus among the people who know early childhood best is that these are not what you should be looking for and could actually be harmful, as you'll see later in the book. However, this doesn't mean that less is better and that preschool programs should simply be a thinned-out, scaled-down version of kindergarten either. Preschool programs must simply be different from programs for any other age group. A good preschool program should give each child from about three to five meaningful, developmentally appropriate and enriching play and learning experiences to enhance his or her individual potential for growth during these early-childhood years.

The National Association for the Education of Young Children is made up of early-childhood educators from all parts of the United States. NAEYC, which has a membership of about sixty-five thousand, sets standards and, in some cases, recommends preschools. Schools that have strong connections with NAEYC tend to have sound developmental programs that fit the profile of what we'll be referring to here as good preschool. This is what NAEYC has to say on the subject of academic programs: "The trend toward early academics . . . is antithetical to what we know about how young children learn. Programs should be tailored to meet the needs of children, rather than expecting children to adjust to a specific program."

THE GREAT DEBATE

Of course, as in other parts of education, there are schools of thought on what a good program is. As a parent you should realize that education is currently in the midst of a great debate about what constitutes good preschool. At the heart of it are questions like: Should children three to five years old be drilling in numbers and letters to prepare them for more rigorous kindergarten? Do young children benefit from this kind of early emphasis on academics? And if your child doesn't have this kind of preschool education, will he or she "fall behind"? Paired with these questions are: Aren't today's kids different? Can't they handle more information?

It may be tempting to believe that we are producing a new type of early bloomer. But the facts say otherwise. The birth canal has not suddenly developed a fast lane. Babies are growing and developing at pretty much the same rate that they developed forty years ago. The Gesell Institute has been for many years a parents' guide to how children grow and learn. The Gesell measurements are used in many school districts to measure children's readiness for school. Recently Gesell published a study of how today's children are developing as compared with children of yesterday. It compared behaviors and skills of two-and-a-half- to six-year-olds of the 1940s with those of children of the 1970s. Here's what the researchers discovered:

Of the fifty-one behaviors Gesell tested, 55 percent occurred at exactly the same age among the 1970s children as among the youngsters tested in 1940. In two instances they occurred later than in 1940. The other 41 percent appeared somewhat earlier among the 1970 group. But in no case was the 1970s group more than six months "ahead" of their peers from 1940. In other words, in spite of *Sesame Street*, TV, academic preschools, and the like, more than half of the behavior of average young children of today marches to much the same developmental drummer as that of the kids of 1940. For example, 1970s youngsters were able to answer one comprehension question correctly at age three, two questions correctly at age three and a half, three questions at four and a half.

There have been slight changes—probably about as much change in behavior as there has been change in the size of babies. But on the average, kids still walk at about the same age, talk at about the same age, and operate according to the same general timetable. There are no great surprises in this generation. In fact, it may be instructive to take a look at what is happening to the superkids, who have been "hothoused" from infancy in intensely pressured academic environments. At four or five they often show signs of stress. In public school they do not always do well. Early pencil-and-paper drill in math and "prereading" does not seem to guarantee a good kindergarten experience or later super performance. Educator David Elkind (author of *The Hurried Child*) believes that the early years are the time to build the desire to learn. He feels that if this early motivational piece is skirted in favor of short-term gains of "facts," a child's later education may very well suffer.

Well-respected educators can be found on both sides of this debate. You'll have to decide for yourself which side you're on before you choose a preschool for your child. Ideally your decision should be based on your own convictions and what your own child is like. But it may be helpful for you to take a look at some of the common ages and stages of preschoolers before you make up your mind.

PRESCHOOL AGES AND STAGES

Every child is one of a kind. Parents and preschool teachers accept and value this idea. At the same time there are certain developmental way stations that seem to occur in most kids. They are good to know for a number of reasons. One is that it's comforting when your child's behavior seems odd to know that the particular oddity is only a stage. It also helps a lot to know something about child development when you start thinking about preschool. It is the background material that will help you make a choice. That is, if you're planning to send a youngster to preschool at three, you'll get more perspective on schools if you learn a little more about what most three-year-olds are like. Then you can decide whether the setting you're looking at has been planned with three-year-olds in mind. You also have to make sure that the program has enough "reach" so that as your three-year-old develops, the program offers other activities tailored to fit his or her greater capabilities at a different stage. In this connection one mother said that she liked her daughter's nursery school for the first year but not the second. "It never changed," she complained. "The next year they were singing the same songs, doing the same puzzles, and playing with the same manipulatives in the same way. This was fine for the newcomers, but for the children who had been there a year it wasn't adequate."

A good preschool program takes into consideration the fact that preschoolers develop at different rates and in different ways, but that there's a general timetable. For this reason, some preschools have two-, three-, four-, and five-year-olds separated, so that they can use the books, toys, and equipment appropriate to their ages and stages. Some settings simply have younger and older groups. Still others have older and younger children separated for certain activities and together for the ones where it is beneficial for both ages. No one way of handling different age groups is always better. In chapter 3 we'll be giving examples of preschools that divide groups in various ways and you can see what way most appeals to you. The important thing is to make sure that the center or nursery school/preschool has materials and activities for all the preschool ages and stages, not just for the youngest or the oldest children and that the teachers are looking at both your child's chronological age and his or her developmental age and is providing individual attention to both.

Here are a few of the common developmental markers for the ages between, roughly, two and a half and five and a half and some of the activities, equipment, and program planning that would be appropriate for these ages and stages. Keep in mind that one whole year's time covers a lot of development and that some children will do some of these things sooner or later in the year, or perhaps even in the previous or the following year. These are general guidelines that are meant only to show the big developmental differences that usually occur from year to year in early childhood.

FROM TWO TO THREE

The hallmark of two and a half to three is large-muscle development. Kids this age know how to both walk and run, but they're trying variations on the theme. So they tend to like to climb and ride toy trucks and open doors and stand on one foot and practice jumping. They love to try things and should have plenty of space to do it. Many preschools provide indoor and outdoor climbing/moving equipment for this age group. But the thing to remember about these young citizens is that they don't have much sense of danger, either for themselves or for other people. Another common developmental trait of two and a half to three is a pretty low frustration level (she gets mad because she can't make the block connection), and judgment isn't always sound (she flings the offending block when there's another child nearby). Knowing the typical behaviors of this age group gives you concrete things to look for in a preschool program for a less-than-three-year-old. Among other things, you'll want to make sure there's good adult supervision as well as safe and adequate outdoor and indoor large-motor play equipment, such as bikes and climbing devices. On this subject, the director of a corporate child care center recently pointed out to me a piece of equipment that she said was going back. ''They told us that the climbing tower had adjustable bars," she fumed. "But they don't adjust well enough for the little ones. They can slip right through. There's no way for the caregiver to watch every side of that tower either. We can't allow our younger children on it."

This experienced educator knows that two-to-three-year-olds explore widely and wildly. She understands from experience Piaget's observation that "this age thinks with actions." But two-to-threes aren't all action, and this, too, needs to be kept in mind when you're looking for a quality preschool setting. Two-to-three-year-olds have sharp powers of observation. They soak up new language and learn an astonishing amount, given a chance to hear stories, look at books, talk to one another, and participate in Circle Time, where everyone in the group is encouraged to join in and talk, even with a few words. This is the time when children can learn the difference between "one" and "many," between a toy chest and the chest that is part of the body. Materials to explore and to talk about experience using language need to be provided for the two-to-three-year-old, who may not be quite ready for small eye-hand tasks and will just about be able to build with a few blocks or cut a little bit with blunt scissors.

Teacher-caregivers of this tender age need also to appreciate the "youngness" of this youngest preschool group. They can't and shouldn't be treated like five-year-olds or even like fours and older threes. They don't understand lengthy lectures about behavior, and they have short attention spans. Because under-three-year-olds can often be both negative and bossy, teachers need to know how to distract without meeting a no head-on. Naps or a rest time are a must for this group. Donna Woehrle, the director of the Phelps Child Care Center, mentions another item on her agenda for two- and three-year-olds: "Frequent snack meals are better for this age group than one or two big meals with nothing in between. Feed young children often is my motto.'' If a preschool is paying attention to development, these are just a few of the things it will take into consideration.

FROM THREE TO FOUR

Three is often spoken of as the ''golden time'' of the preschool years. Indeed, the three-year-old does seem at peace with himself and the world. Three-year-olds may go off to preschool with a minimum of separation anxiety about leaving their parents. While they are with other children, they play more sociably than they did earlier. Three-year-olds approaching four master all kinds of small hand movements. They can pick up tiny objects, such as raisins, and they can hold a paintbrush and can sometimes draw a stick figure. Puzzles, too, are easier for them now, and most of them can fit pegs into small holes. Because they're more able to make their wishes known, they're less apt to have temper tantrums of frustration, and they can work on a task such as block building with other children in a more cooperative way.

And three-to-four-year-olds have a rich fantasy life. This is the age of the imaginary friend, the ''pretend'' store, the dress-up hat. At the same time, threes and fours are graduating to more sophisticated outdoor climbing. Some of them can manage a balance beam or the jungle bars.

You can see by this description that children need some different preschool materials and experiences when they reach this age/stage. A dress-up corner and puppets are ''musts'' to feed this age group's imaginative life; creative fantasy play is one of the cornerstones of problem-solving skills, according to such experts as Dr. Jerome Singer.

Children of this age are much more apt to use crayons and paints for longer periods of time. Circle Time is a time of talking in full sentences. At three, preschool teachers can expect that routines such as hand washing or picking up toys can be followed with some consistency, and simple instructions ("First you turn the paper shiny side up, then you put the finger paint on") can be followed.

To be in sync with three-to-four-year-olds is to allow them to be a little more independent. Materials and activities should be available that feed their longer attention span. These may in some cases be the same materials they used at two to three, but now they use them in new ways. Some almost-four-year-olds can build real block constructions. On the academic side, three- and four-year-olds often can count a little, and some of them recognize a few letters, particularly the letters in their names. For this reason, books are a staple of every preschool program, and for this age group there should also be lots of signs around the nursery school or child care center, so that children of three to four can see a variety of letters and words. The children who are developmentally ready will respond if someone says, "Find the cubby that has your name on it." One teacher said, "Some children love to 'write,' even when they're only three and can only make scribbles. Because they're so interested and because the crayons and fat pencils are there, they get the feel of holding a writing instrument. I never correct a child or insist that he do it a certain way. As they get older, they get more control."

The real message here is that you make all tools of learning available. Most three-to-four-year-olds are developmentally ready to hear longer stories and to match up simple shapes. They like and appreciate rhymes; some they can remember. Some of them will know a few colors, but they have a limited understanding of color. Here's an example: In one preschool I visited, the children were playing with transparent plastic color paddles. There were red, blue, and yellow paddles—one for each primary color. By putting them over each other you get the secondary colors —blue over red gives purple, blue over yellow gives green, and so on. I was talking with some three-to-four-year-olds who knew the color of each paddle. They also knew the color green in another toy. Yet when I put the blue paddle over the yellow one and asked what color it was, they all said blue. The thing is, they knew the paddle on the top was blue from experience. They were not developmentally ready to accept what they saw and modify what they already "knew." Somewhat later I went over to the oldest boy in the group, who is nearly five. When I played the same game with him, he immediately said that the color he saw was green.

Color paddles are toys that both threes and fours can get something out of, but perhaps in different ways. And a good preschool teacher will know that it is counterproductive to try to make a three-year-old learn what he's not ready to understand.

From age three on, having a live pet in the room can be a rewarding experience. This is science in its most delightful guise, and the fact that kids can have the experience with proper adult supervision eliminates many of the problems that can crop up keeping a pet at home. Whether it's a rabbit, goldfish, or guinea pig, preschool children can share meaningful observations as well as the care with adults standing by to make sure that both child and animal are protected and that no one child has responsibilities for the pet that are beyond his capabilities.

Three-and-a-half-to-four-year-olds enjoy going on trips in the neighborhood. They are very observant if asked to look for certain things (all the things that are red or are circles, for instance) although some can focus on such a job only as they approach four.

FROM FOUR TO FIVE

Four-to-five-year-olds seem endlessly curious and enthusiastic about everything. Some of the staples of good preschool—such as the block corner, the easel, and Lego sets —are still used by this older group, but they're used in different ways. The block buildings they make are higher and more complex, and elaborate discussions may go along with the constructions. Four- and five-year-olds may sometimes build something to fit a game they're playing. Beginning around four, many children can handle buttons on their clothes. They can follow directions, which means that they can have some small responsibilities in preschool and at home. The four-to-five-year-old is so responsive and so quick to catch on that she is able to participate in cooking, playing a simple Lotto game, even perhaps taking attendance if all the names are written on a board.

It is precisely because four-to-five-year-olds seem to be so receptive to all kinds of learning that trouble can start. They are so eager to learn that it's tempting to push. Just because a child shows a tendency toward print awareness does not mean he should immediately be pressured into reading readiness programs and a barrage of pencil-and-paper activities. It may seem that pencil-and-worksheet work is an appropriate way to use that window of developmental opportunity that we spoke of earlier. But in fact, there is a good deal of evidence that most youngsters (particularly boys) need unstructured time with books and other readiness materials between first becoming print aware and actually learning to read (see page 184). Quality preschool not only makes sure that children get enough stimulation at each stage but that they don't get so much in only a few "academic" areas that other equally valuable developmental lessons of growing are lost.

If your child is four or more, make sure that the preschool you choose looks at the whole four-to-five-year-old. A good program for fours and fives will include portable outdoor and/or indoor equipment that can be rearranged by the children themselves to satisfy the adventurousness that's a hallmark of this age. There should be plenty of sorting, matching, and classifying games available, such as attribute blocks and sequence cards. In the Bank Street Lower School, teachers invent counting and sorting games with their own materials. One teacher has a collection of bottle caps, which are used for matching as well as sorting and counting, and provide the extra fun of being artifacts children may recognize. These are most valuable learning tools, as are concept books, sensory material, and very simple hands-on science experiments (cooking, for example). And children of four to five are extremely curious about their bodies. The songs, games, and records that help children learn about their body parts are fun, but they are a part of good nursery curriculum because they also serve a developmentally appropriate function. They teach children what they need to know when they're ready for it.

This is also true of language learning. Four-to-five-year-olds in a nursery or preschool are ready to talk about many things and in full sentences. Discussion time for fours and fives in a developmentally oriented preschool is rich with all kinds of language learning. Many times the teacher starts the ball rolling and then the youngsters take over. Circle Time, when it's done right, is a social time of both sharing ideas and expressing opinions. "What do you think?" is a wonderful and powerful question for a four-to-five-year-old to answer. It can be asked about any number of everyday issues and it doesn't require a right-or-wrong answer. To answer requires vocabulary, reasoning, organization, comprehension, and a few other skills as well. That's a lot for a four-to-five-year-old, but many of them can handle it.

THE FIVE-YEAR-OLD

At five many children are today entering kindergarten. Some children are developmentally ready, some are not. This is perhaps one of the most puzzling and frustrating times for many parents, especially since schools have different ways of evaluating ''readiness.'' Some schools concentrate on academic skills while others look at social or emotional maturity. Few schools can make ready for children at different stages rather than asking the children to become ready for the school.

Many children who are bright and capable learners have not yet developed some of the maturity they need for a typical kindergarten program. Sometimes they have all the letters and numbers down pat but are not able to sit still long enough to get much from the usual kindergarten programs. They may have trouble holding a pencil, they may be lagging in language or social skills. The months between five and six are very important growing months in many ways and they shouldn't be rushed. Perhaps the most important gift a parent can give a five-to-six-year-old may be ample opportunity to grow and learn at his or her own rate. One excellent question to ask your school district is how it measures ''readiness'' and whether it works with the preschools in evaluating a child. In chapter 10 we discuss this very special stage and what the transition from preschool to kindergarten means to you and to your child.

To sum up:

▲ Each child is a unique person. That means that your child's learning pattern and growth may be different from other children's and still follow a general predictable sequence.

• Young children from two to five don't learn from symbols as much as they learn from concrete experiences. That means that they learn more from touching things and moving them around and fooling with them than they do from being pushed into prereading and number activities.

▪ All children need to learn to use their bodies. They also need to be comfortable with their own bodies and physical capabilities. While this may seem like incidental learning, it's not. Control over one's body seems to strongly influence other areas of learning. Children who practice control of their body movements gain confidence and independence. Conversely, kids who are confined at table tasks for long periods of time or who are pressed to play games or sports that are too hard for them sometimes lag later in areas unconnected to physical play.

▲ Children learn from other children as well as from parents and teachers. Social skills are among the great benefits of preschool learning. Learning to get along with others has a decided effect on home behavior, on personality development, and on later school success.

• Children change rapidly from ages two to five. Parents and teachers need to be aware of and adjust to these changes. A good preschool program tailors its curriculum to fit each individual as well as each age group. This is one of the reasons why small groups work better than large ones.

▪ Children learn in stages. Good preschools create an

environment where a child can go through all the stages of learning rather than being rushed into academic skills without a proper foundation.

THE THREE-WAY PARTNERSHIP

A good preschool experience means a lot of things. Naturally it means a good setting, a quality program, a proper match between school and child. It means a healthy mix of the physical and intellectual and a chance for a child to grow socially and to move toward independence. It means enjoying the ''now'' of preschool, not merely as a passage and preparation for kindergarten but as a separate, unique, and rich event. But there's another factor that, perhaps more than any other, makes good preschool happen. It is the vital chemistry and communication—the partnership—among the parties. This is probably the core of preschool as well as of this book. We'll be talking about it in many contexts and we'll be looking at most preschool issues from three perspectives—parent, child, and teacher.

CHILD AS PARTNER

First is the child. The child's view is important and needs to be considered. After all, whose preschool experience is it, anyway?

A little personal hindsight here may be useful. When my older child was three, he started nursery school for half a day. He started at the same time as a friend's child and, in fact, I chose the school on my friend's recommendation. We walked to the school together every morning. Her child was happy from the first day and paid her mom no mind after the first five minutes. My son was miserable and clung to me every day for weeks. I remember feeling embarrassed. Why couldn't he adjust, the way J's child had? What was I doing wrong? The fact was, my youngster never enjoyed going to that preschool. In the light of what I now know about preschools, I think it was not a bad place but it was far from ideal. And it certainly was wrong for him. I wish I had paid more attention to what my son was trying to tell me and had looked around for a better match between my child and the school, rather than taking my friend's child as a model.

A parent may say, "But a three- or four-year-old isn't old enough to have opinions that can help make preschool work." Young children certainly can't express feelings as well as grownups can. And they can't make final decisions. But they certainly can be involved in the choice of preschool. They need to be prepared for this change in their lives and to be introduced to new settings. In decisions that impact on children, an understanding parent can pick up clues about what a youngster may not be able to put into words. Children send messages with their behavior as well as their language. That's where a child comes into the vital partnership. We deal with this idea further in chapter 5.

Today's children are bound to be affected by the change in family patterns. Sometimes they are going to have to make bigger adjustments in their lives at younger ages. Many of them may cope with frequent moves from one place to another or from one child care center to another. Others live part of the time with one parent, part of the time with another or with a stepparent or live-in surrogate father or mother. Some children seldom see their fathers, while some see more of their dads than they do of their mothers. Others see their parents only at night and on weekends. And many more children are in the care of other people who, in some cases, are as close to the children as their parents are.

These new patterns are not necessarily bad. They're just different. The result of some of them is that, in general, children are required to be more independent earlier. Their parents want them to be. This argues for children being active partners in the preschool experience, even at an early age. In other words, preschool shouldn't be simply something that happens to a child. It should happen *with* the child. He or she needs to have input and, in fact, in the best preschools the program itself grows out of this idea. The child, after all, is what preschool is all about.

We talked with a lot of youngsters in preschools. We watched their behavior and we listened to what they had to say to other children and to their teachers. We tried to interpret some of their feelings about school and we got feedback about what they were doing and saying from their parents and teachers. In a few cases, we saw children who weren't happy, and most of the time it was pretty obvious why. (You'll find these issues addressed in later chapters.) In other words, the children described and quoted here are not child development statistics but real children, male and female. We've used *he* or *she* for specific children, but in most cases the anecdotes are not gender related.

PARENT AS PARTNER

Parents—all parents—have a tremendous amount to contribute to making preschool successful. Every single study of quality early childhood centers, preschools, and nursery schools suggests that the best ones are the ones that have, among other things, a strong parent component. Educators all agree on the fact that preschool programs are more successful when parents participate. It is a truism that children get more out of preschool when they see and feel the fact that their mother or father or both parents support their school and its activities. This is true in later school as well. (One of the most consistent predictors of children's educational achievement in elementary school is parental support.)

This doesn't mean that parents necessarily have to work at the preschool, or even that they need to come to the preschool or center on a regular basis. It simply means that parents should be involved in some visible, consistent way —for example, by going to parent-teacher conferences, attending parent meetings and/or parties, talking with a child about specific aspects of his or her experiences.

The parent partnership is obviously good for the child. If you know what's going on, you can bring school and home together and extend the good things that are happening. But it's also good for you, the parent. Preschool is a place where parents as well as children get a little schooling. No one knows everything about parenting, and given today's tight schedules, many parents don't have the time to take courses or join workshops. It is comforting to be able to talk to someone when a parenting question or problem comes up. In a good preschool the resources are all there—other parents to share experiences and questions with and professional educators who can sometimes be a model of ''how to'' and at other times an understanding listener or counselor.

Parents as partners also help the teacher. When parents keep in touch with teacher and center, the teacher and preschool can do a better job. When parents share with teachers and keep the lines of communication open, it works for the benefit of the child. It's a sort of circle effect —what goes around comes around, as you will see in many examples in later chapters.

We had contact with parents of preschoolers in a number of different settings, through personal interviews and through a questionnaire. From the answers we got to our modest survey, it seems that parents of today want very much to be good parents, to help their children as much as possible in every way they can. Concern for offspring cuts across all socioeconomic, gender, and ethnic lines. Most parents, regardless of background and circumstances, want to do a good job of raising their children. And they're willing to go the extra mile for this goal, even though they may have less time than they've ever had. In quality preschool, parents can get what they so much seem to want—a chance to participate in their child's experience and to learn more about being a parent.

TEACHER AS PARTNER

A preschool can only be as good as its teachers and its director. Studies show that quality preschools are much more likely to have teachers who are well trained and well paid and who have specific early childhood training. Teachers shape the programs of preschool, and well-trained, experienced teachers who know how children learn and develop can give special meaning to each individual child's needs.

At this particular time, child care/preschool settings are changing in many ways. There are beginning to be more choices, and the need for better-trained teachers and directors has been identified. Where teachers don't have specific early childhood credentials, they often have extensive on-the-job training. And any teacher who has been in preschool education recognizes the benefits of working together with parents for the good of the child. The most valuable thing about a teacher is his or her trained eye. Because teachers see so many children of a certain age, they tend to recognize common growth patterns. This can be very comforting to a parent who thinks her youngster is going through some bizarre stage. Being in touch with the teacher, sharing thoughts about the child, can be both comforting and rewarding. Teachers aren't always right, but certainly two heads are better than one.

The teachers we interviewed all mentioned working together with parents. Sometimes they brought it up even before we did. They want to work with parents. They want to be in touch. They plan parent meetings and conferences carefully and try to set up strong home-to-school and school-to-home connections. Although in a few cases teachers were critical of parents and said they felt that their work with the children was not being sufficiently supported, they all thought that more communication might change their views. And they all felt that getting information from home about the child and what was going on was an important element of preschool.

SOME GOOD REASONS FOR A CHILD TO GO TO PRESCHOOL

1. To encourage self-identity (a life of his or her own).

2. To promote self-reliance and independence.

3. To gain mastery of basic rules and routines.

4. To develop language and communicate more effectively.

5. To provide exposure to books, art, and play materials that may not be available at home.

6. To meet and learn to get on with other children.

7. To practice using his or her body effectively.

8. To improve fine motor skills.

9. To enjoy freedom of action in a place designed and geared to his or her age.

10. To become closely acquainted with warm, caring adults outside the family.

SOME NOT-SO-GOOD REASONS FOR A CHILD TO GO TO PRESCHOOL

1. Everyone is doing it.

2. The child lacks discipline or is having problems.

3. It will give the child a fast start on academics for kindergarten.

4. The child is too attached to you.

SOME GOOD REASONS NOT TO SEND A CHILD TO PRESCHOOL

1. You're enjoying having your youngster around and you're not quite ready to give that up, even for half a day.

2. Good preschool in your area is expensive and you can't afford it.

3. Your child has plenty of opportunities to play and socialize with other children.

4. Your youngster doesn't want to go.

5. You don't like the preschools in your area.

6. You feel you and your spouse are providing your youngster with good preschool experiences.

CHOOSING
A PRESCHOOL

"Begin at the beginning," says the King in *Alice in Wonderland*. The beginning of good preschool is making the right choice. And a good choice is not always the most expensive, the trendiest, or even the best-looking school. What you're looking for is a setting that fits your own needs and those of your child. You want a preschool that is generally based on your own child-rearing ideas and practices, so that there is some agreement about what is important. To find it, you have to ask yourself who you are, who your child is, what you want for all of you, and what kind of place and what kind of teachers are most likely to give it to you. Surprisingly, it has less to do with physical appearance than you'd think.

One of your first tasks is to make decisions on some basics. Here are a few of the questions you'll want to mull over.

PRESCHOOL PHILOSOPHIES

An overwhelming number of parents we interviewed said that their top priority in choosing a preschool was the school's basic philosophy. Some parents had a pretty clear idea of what they wanted their children to get from preschool. A few had special requirements—that the school have a religious base or multi-ethnic focus—and that made it easier for them in choosing. It's a little harder to recognize the *philosophy* of a school at first glance, but there are, roughly, three models, which we'll call A, B, and C.

A. CHILD-CENTERED

In this kind of setting, the cues for what happens during a day come largely from the children. For instance, there's no set painting time—a child paints when she feels like it, explores with blocks for as long or as short a period as she likes. If a group of children become interested in something (such as a sudden snowfall), the teacher may facilitate their talk and play around that theme, but mostly they're on their own. In a true child-centered setting, a child discovers and learns through his own use of the setting and materials and through play with his peers, with little instruction or formal guidance from the teacher. In all good nursery/preschool settings, children learn through play, but in a child-centered school, the play is quite free-wheeling. You'll see children building with blocks or playing house or reading books or watching the live rabbits, as they feel like it. The atmosphere in a child-centered preschool can be anything, from pleasantly relaxed hubbub to noisy confusion.

The best thing about a child-centered preschool is the fact that it accepts the idea that young children learn through play, and it usually has developmentally appropriate materials around for them to play with. Children probably have more freedom in a child-centered atmosphere, and many youngsters seem to thrive in this kind of setting, developing their own priorities and a sense of independence. Other children seem to need more structure than this kind of setup generally provides. The key factor in a child-centered program is both how comfortable your child is with it and how you personally feel about it. Certainly many nursery schools are at least partly child-centered.

B. TEACHER-DIRECTED

At the opposite end of the spectrum is the teacher-directed preschool. In this kind of setting, the activities of the day are planned and carried out by the teachers. Play itself may have a more formal cast, with the teacher leading discussions and often asking questions that require a specific response. ''What color is this?'' ''How many fingers do I have up?'' A teacher-directed program obviously requires tighter discipline in order to function, so in this preschool you'll see less free play, less individual activities or small groups working independently. The children may actually be doing pencil-and-paper activities sitting at desks. Art may consist of everyone pasting or cutting the same shape from a model made by the teacher. There's usually a set routine for when things happen, as well as what happens.

If you're looking at a B preschool, you'll often get the sensation of a classroom rather than a nursery. The literature of this kind of school may stress academic or kindergarten preparation, and the emphasis will clearly be on *teaching* preschoolers, in contrast to A, which would give them the space in which to play and learn on their own.

C. DEVELOPMENTAL OR DEVELOPMENTAL-INTERACTIONIST

Developmental schools are based on the development principles we've already outlined—age-appropriate play, activities, and materials. Neither teacher-directed nor entirely child-centered, they're settings where teachers and children enjoy a sort of learn/play partnership. Sometimes the kids initiate activities and the teachers help to extend them and make them richer. Sometimes the teachers initiate activities appropriate for the children's ages. In this type of setting you'll see young people exercising outdoors, painting, planting seeds, modeling with clay, playing dress-up, singing, building with blocks, experimenting with shape puzzles, listening to stories, and talking about all sorts of things with their teachers. Through these activities they'll be learning (among other things) prereading and premath concepts. Most importantly, you'll notice that the teachers at a child care center of this type treat the boys and girls as individuals and that many of the activities that take place flow from what the children do or talk about.

Here's a capsule illustration of some of the differences between pure A, B, and C schools. Let's imagine a talk between a teacher and a group of children. In a child-centered (A) school, a teacher will listen attentively to what the children have to say about something that interests them, but she probably won't seize the moment to extend the talk or to direct them to an activity that explores the subject further.

In a teacher-directed (B) preschool, the teacher will organize and direct the discussion. She will often pick the subject herself and prepare questions that test the children's knowledge of facts and require a specific answer. Obviously, this requires tighter control over the class and more quiet behavior.

In a developmental-interactive preschool, the teacher may pick up on what a group of youngsters is talking about. She may guide the discussion, keeping an eye on the attention span of the group and trying to draw everyone into the talk. Her questions may be on the order of ''What do you think?'' or ''Let's try that and see what happens,'' rather than more specific yes-no, true-false questions.

THE BLURRED EDGES

The truth is, there probably are very few pure A's, B's, and C's. What's out there is usually a mix, with a predilection toward one or the other style. An individual teacher's style can weight a program a little bit one way or the other. Many preschools today incorporate the basics of sound developmental philosophy. To the extent that they do, they are by definition child-centered, in that they watch the child for cues as to what material and activity are appropriate. On the other hand, the same school may also assign importance to the role of the teacher—as mentor, as catalyst, and as guide. Bank Street School calls its educational philosophy developmental-interactionist, which acknowledges the fact that it is based on the interaction of child and teacher, with the child's developmental needs the drive and the teacher's understanding of those needs and her recognition of individual differences the response.

If, as in the proverbial Chinese menu, you could pick something from column A, B, and C, and put them all together, you might get, for example, a Montessori school.

Montessori schools are, in a sense, child-centered. But they're certainly not loosely structured; in fact, in Montessori schools a tight discipline is imposed through the specificity of the materials and through the teacher acting as mentor. In other words, the child is the center, but his or her activities are controlled by the materials. Montessori schools are developmentally oriented, but they interpret developmental signals in different ways from, for instance, a C school. In some Montessori schools children start to learn reading, math, and writing at four, often with older children as "teachers."

MAKING YOUR CHOICE

It's good to know different ways of categorizing preschool programs, not so much because you are going to find these exact models but because it gives you a general idea of what to look for and what you're looking at. You can ask more informed questions and observe with a clearer eye. Keep in mind that parent involvement is a key factor in *all* quality preschool programs, whether they are A, B, C or a mix. The most important aspect of knowing the direction of a school is in terms of your child. Children may develop within similar time frames, but each one is unique. Make sure that you pick a school that your child can be comfortable in and one where you can be an active partner in his or her school life.

Are you looking for an all-day preschool program or a half-day or part-time program? If your child is under three and you can possibly manage it, a half-day preschool program is certainly enough, and possibly preferable. In visiting preschools and child care centers, it seemed to me that often children younger than three (or even in some cases older) didn't have the stamina to go through a whole day of nursery school. Some of them seemed cranky or dazed by the end of the day. Mothers and fathers I spoke with testified to the fact that the under-threes sometimes had trouble coping with the long day.

If your child is older than three, you may still prefer a part-time program. If you absolutely must have all-day care for your child, one way around the all-day preschool dilemma may be for you and your partner to share the care temporarily. Try to juggle your work times so that one of you is home for the extra hours, at least until your youngster is ready for preschool for the whole day. Another strategy is to have backup baby-sitters for the time between pickup at preschool and your arrival at home. But keep in mind that these layered arrangements add one more level of complexity to your life. You have to weigh them against what may be the strain of a full day in preschool for your child.

Knowing what a youngster can tolerate in terms of time is tricky. At one end of the spectrum is the boy or girl who violates general developmental rules by having great staying power at an early age. At the other end is the child for whom three hours a day away from home is plenty all the way through kindergarten. Here's where your own instincts about your child, coupled with sensitive observation and advice by the preschool director, can help you make an informed judgment. A suggestion: if you must send your child to preschool all day, start with a few hours and gradually increase the time (especially if he's on the young side) ; see how he fares. Many preschools will allow you to adjust your hours up or down to a certain extent, although few programs will want you to bring your child there for three hours one day and eight hours the next. Many educators feel that children get more out of a part-time program every day than a full-time program for part of the week.

A teacher relaxes with a group of preschoolers in Bank Street's after-school program.

The time factor is inseparable from the kind of program you choose. If you intend to put a young child in a full-day preschool program, the last hours should surely be "downtime" (more of this on page 144). John Regis, who teaches in Bank Street's afterschool preschool program, which runs from 3:30 to about 6:30, thinks that one planned activity for the shank of the day is plenty. "We might talk about fruit and make a fruit drink in the blender—something like that. The kids are ready to slow down. A few lie down. Once or twice a child has actually fallen asleep. By the time they come to us, they've already had a pretty full day, so we provide one focused activity for those who may want it—the rest of them we help to relax."

THE COST ISSUE

Money is another issue that must be central to your thinking about preschool. It has to figure prominently in your plans and may even be linked to the time factor (maybe you can only stretch the budget for half-day preschool).

Paid full-time preschool costs about $40 to $49 a week on average. In Atlanta, Georgia, fees run from $35 to $70; in New York City parents are paying $50 to $150. Weekly fees for half-day preschool or full-time preschool for part of the week are comparably less. One corporate center we visited charges its employees $480 a month for preschoolers, while outside families pay $100 a month more. This may sound like a great deal of money, but when you consider that this center's doors open at 6:30 in the morning and close at 8:00 at night, this preschool costs about $3 an hour—less than what a baby-sitter charges these days.

To get a realistic picture of costs for your own situation, break them down in terms of a week or a month or whatever way you figure your budget. Look at cost-to-salary ratio and compare the cost of preschool to your present child care costs, if you have any. If you're working, keep in mind that some of the costs of preschool can earn tax credits. On this basis, you may decide you can handle it, you may feel that you can afford half-day but not full-day preschool, or you may decide that the advantages of preschool are not worth the financial drain. One thing is certain—it takes a hefty family budget to handle the costs of full-time private preschool. And it doesn't do anyone in the family much good if a child's going to preschool gives her parents money worries.

Be sure you look at all your options before you decide you can't afford to send your child to preschool. Community preschools (like those operated and sponsored by YMCAs, church groups, and so on) have either a sliding scale of fees based on income or lower fees because they're nonprofit. They may have a scholarship fund that can help families who can't quite afford preschool. Another way to deal with the money issue is by looking for a co-op pre-school. Co-ops are run on a nonprofit basis and sometimes get grants from community sources, so they can set lower fees. Co-ops can often make a go of it because they use parents as a resource. In one co-op I know of, the parents built much of the outdoor equipment, did the indoor painting and maintenance, and act as aides on a rotating basis. Some co-ops ask you to trade work time with the school in exchange for lower fees. Others ask all the parents to put in an equal amount of contributed time toward scholarships for needier families.

Sleepy Hollow Co-op in Marin County, California, is a parent cooperative of this type. At Sleepy Hollow about twelve four-year-olds attend preschool for about two and a half hours on Mondays, Wednesdays, and Fridays. Younger children go on Tuesdays and Thursdays. The head teacher at Sleepy Hollow has early childhood credentials. The rest of the staff is made up of parents who take turns being with the groups. According to Bill and Wendy Dreskin, whose daughter, Leila, goes to the school, all the parents are highly motivated, even if they don't have professional experience as educators. Monthly meetings are held for discussion of the preschool's program, which is an easygoing blend of crafts, creativity, and sociability.

The atmosphere in a cooperative nursery or preschool can be wonderful. Certainly the spirit is very much in tune with the idea of a partnership among school, child, and parent. You could make a pretty good case for a cooperative preschool even if you don't have a fiscal reason. The big contribution you make in a co-op is to commit a certain parcel of time. Before you go the co-op route, you have to decide whether you can do that.

As we mentioned earlier, Head Start and the new pre-K programs are both free. However, either one may be hard to get into. Many of these programs only target at-risk or handicapped children, and the waiting list is long. There are only a few public school initiatives that are open to all children. One example is the Hewlitt-Woodmere, Long Island, pre-K program (see chapter 10), which fills the bill for a middle-class as well as a poor family with preschoolers.

Make up your mind at the outset what you can afford to spend. That will determine whether you're headed for the private, community, public, or co-op route. Then gather the information about the sector you have chosen.

LARGE VERSUS SMALL SETTINGS

What if there are several preschools in your neighborhood and they have similar programs? One is part of a large chain, the other is a small setting. Should size be a factor in your choice?

The size of the group your child is in is more important than the size of the whole place (the setting). In other words, let's say there are 110 children in a child care center, with 40 preschoolers, divided into three groups, in separate rooms. The group your child will be in, four-year-olds, has 15 children and two teachers. This is a good group size, as you'll see from the chart on page 69. Group size being equal, a somewhat larger setting may give you certain other advantages, in terms of specialist contacts (psychologist, speech therapist, and the like) or food service. If it is a setting where they also care for infants and toddlers or have a school for older children, there's the opportunity for your youngster to see and play with both older and younger children. Some preschools consider this interaction a significant part of the program. Whether you are going to have a baby in your house soon or whether your child is an only, being around a baby or toddler may be a valuable part of her preschool education.

But a small setting also can have advantages. Here the atmosphere will tend to be more like an extended family. A nursery school that has a total of only 20 or 30 children may be a cozier setting for a child who takes longer to warm up, provided the group size is the same as in the larger center. The chance for the director to get to know each child is certainly greater. She's learning only 30 names and faces instead of 110. Teacher-parent interaction may be more intimate, too, and you may have a better chance of getting quick and direct action on a specific problem. A smaller setting may suit a younger or more immature child. Ask yourself whether the size of the place affects the overall program and which setting your child seems to be most comfortable in.

When to Start Looking

How far ahead should you start shopping for a preschool? One worried mother, galvanized into action by stories about the crunch for a place in preschool, started shopping for a preschool when she got pregnant. While this parent may have been a little premature in her search, it's well to keep in mind that in some locations there is a dearth of good preschools and you will feel some pressure to get a place in line.

In large metropolitan areas such as Chicago, child care agencies recommend that you start right after Labor Day of the year before you plan to send your child. This means, of course, that you will have to lay out a nonrefundable deposit, and in reality it may not guarantee you the teachers you saw and liked. However, in a situation where the choice is between a deposit on a school you want and taking a chance on losing the game of preschool musical chairs, you should probably make your move.

The crunch is not quite so noticeable outside the big cities, particularly if you are going the private or community preschool route. Debby, a neighbor of mine, moved back to our rural area when she separated from her husband. She works part-time as a beautician and was looking for a preschool for three-year-old Brandy that wasn't too expensive and had flexible hours. She told me that she found what she was looking for within six weeks. The same thing is true of Leda, another friend, who lives in suburban New York State. Both women, incidentally, made their final choice from among three good nursery schools. And both said their final decision was based on which setting their child seemed most comfortable in.

However, one of the difficulties you may face when you shop preschool way in advance is making an accurate match between child and preschool. You can certainly decide which general mode of preschool you prefer. But given children's ages and stages, you may have a little trouble evaluating how your youngster will ''fit'' into a specific preschool program when the time comes for him or her to start. In this case, you may want to make a special effort to check into the continuity at the preschool: how stable the staff is and how long the director has been there. This will help you to get a picture of whether the preschool will be essentially the same when your child is ready to start.

WHERE TO LOOK

You could be one of those lucky parents who hear about the perfect preschool through the grapevine—a tip from a friend or colleague. You might be fortunate enough to have a good preschool setting at your job. But most likely you'll have to scout around.

Before you start letting your fingers wander through the Yellow Pages, you should check out those whose opinions you trust. Ask relatives, friends, your religious leader, your pediatrician. Friends from the park can be a help; many a good preschool has been found through a playground acquaintance.

There's a growing trend toward privately sponsored nonprofit child care that is available through community agencies. Often these settings can be reached by looking under the local government telephone listing and then under "Child." They're the logical next step if you live in a suburb or a rural area and you've exhausted the personal contacts. If you live in a large city, go directly to the Yellow Pages and look under schools or nursery schools. Here's a checklist of sources:

Relatives and friends

Your pediatrician

Referral services at your job

Child care councils and resources and referral services (the Yellow Pages)

Religious organizations

Children and family service agencies, such as the YMCA and YMHA

Local city and state agencies

INQUIRIES

If you're shopping for a coat or a microwave, it's easy to set your sights on just what you want. Shopping for a preschool is quite different. What you want when you select care and education for your child involves the practical considerations already mentioned, put together with your own philosophy of child rearing. You want a preschool that *feels* right to you and to your child and you don't want to be overly influenced by cute murals on the walls or by a persuasive director.

After you zero in on a few specific names, you're ready to make phone calls. It is a good idea to have a list of "first" questions to ask on the phone. Your list may go something like this:

▲ *What ages do you service?* This will tell you immediately whether your child is eligible for this particular program.

• *Is there an opening for a child my child's age?* If there isn't, ask how long the waiting list is.

▪ *Is your setting licensed?* Most states require some form of licensing for nursery schools and child care centers, but the requirements for licensing vary. The fact that a place has a license doesn't guarantee quality care. But what a license can do is assure you of minimum health and safety standards—number of exits, general cleanliness, first-aid equipment in place. (More about this later.)

▲ *What hours of care do you offer?* This helps you to determine whether the center fits your particular needs. You should never put a child in preschool hoping to "work out" a different schedule later, unless the program is set up for that option.

• *How large are your class groups?* Group size, as we've said, is an important predictor of quality. Even where there's a good ratio of teachers to children, young children simply get more out of preschool when they're in a smaller rather than a larger group. If you can possibly find quality preschool where the groups of three-year-olds are smaller than fifteen and the fours and fives no larger than eighteen, it may be worth giving up some of your other requirements.

▪ *Where is your school located?* You may have to rule out a place that's too far away or figure out whether it is worth it to go the extra distance because everything else sounds good. If the school comes highly recommended, you may be able to arrange transportation, but you need to think about your youngster and whether the trip will be too much for him or her. This is a judgment call on your part.

▲ *What are your fees?* This may be a key question for you, in which case you should move it up to the top of your list. At the same time you should find out whether there are scholarships, subsidies, or a sliding fee scale.

THE SCHOOL BROCHURE

You may have already gotten a brochure before you made your phone call. If not, you'll want to ask for one before you hang up the phone if the preschool sounds promising. Or, if the place is in the neighborhood, you may want to go and pick one up right away. Written information from a preschool should spell out its goals and philosophy. It should clarify for you what kind of program it has and what the facilities are like. But most importantly, the brochure should give you a sense of what the preschool thinks is appropriate for young children. Two brochures I saw recently were in direct contrast to each other. One emphasized equipment—it stressed the fact that the setting had computers, that it had "literacy toys," and that it "prepared children for kindergarten." The pictures showed children sitting in front of computer screens. The other brochure emphasized small group settings, indoor and outdoor play, and teachers with specific early childhood experience. It showed pictures of children cooking and painting and crawling in and out of big outdoor mazes. This one didn't say a thing about preparing a child for kindergarten, but it is likely that it is doing just that in another, and perhaps better, way.

Clearly, if you don't want a setting that stresses academics, you would not be attracted by the first brochure. And you'll want to think more than twice about a school that raves in their brochure about ''extras,'' such as music or karate lessons. These are not only not important components of a nursery or preschool, they are inappropriate activities for most young children. Roberta Altman, who teaches movement to Bank Street preschoolers, puts it this way : ''Children need to learn to use their own bodies first, before they put an extension on them, whether it's a tennis racket or a violin bow. And they need to learn the general rules of getting along in preschool before they can learn the specific rules of a sport like karate.'' The fact that a school features them in its literature may mean that they don't have some of the other more basic aspects of good early childhood education.

One other way to get a feel for what goes on in a preschool day-to-day is to ask to see the most recent parent newsletter or the weekly communication that is sent home with the children. This is generally less formal than the brochure and may help you to decide whether you want to pay the center or school a visit.

LICENSING

Find out if your city or state has licensing requirements and just what they mean. If a school you visit isn't required to have a state license, you'll have to set up your own ''licensing requirements.'' One of the most important is the ratio of children to staff. Equally important is the total number of children in the group. The following is a good guide:

AGES	NUMBER OF TEACHERS	MAXIMUM SIZE OF GROUP
2-3	Teacher for each 5 children	10
3-4	Teacher for each 7 children	15
4-5	Teacher for each 10 children	20
5-6	Teacher for each 13 children (or 1 teacher and 1 assistant)	25

Another important item is the training of the director. Don't be shy. Ask about credentials. The director of a preschool should be specially trained in early childhood education (preferably with a master's degree) and with a minimum of two years' experience *teaching* young children. We think it important for all the teachers to have professional early childhood training or, at the very least, comparable experience. In most cases, it's the teachers rather than the director who will be spending the most time with your child. It's a kind of truism that a preschool program is only as good as the teachers and director.

Assistant teachers should be mature (nineteen or older) and have at least a high school education and some training. It is important to meet and assess the aides as well as the teachers. They will be spending a good deal of time with your youngster. Be sure to ask how aides are recruited and how long the average aide stays. Many centers and preschools hire students, usually from the education departments of colleges and universities. This is a healthy idea, but it does generally mean that there's a turnover of personnel. If this is true of the preschool you are looking at, make sure that at least the teachers tend to remain. "What is your staff turnover?" is an important question for a first interview. A school that has a rotating director and a different staff every year is not going to give your child an ideal preschool experience.

VISITING PRESCHOOLS

Once you decide that a certain school is a possibility, the next step is to see it in action. Seeing is believing when it comes to preschool programs. That's why the visits (I recommend three) are so important.

Look for a program that welcomes your visits and/or suggests that you visit several times. Don't drop into the setting unannounced the first time. Make an appointment so that the director can spend some time with you.

Ideally, both parents should visit the preschool you're considering. If you can't do it at the same time, then go separately. Single and divorced spouses should try to get the former partner involved in the choice if it's at all possible, especially if the partner is bearing some of the costs and spends time with the child. The links between parent, child, and preschool are much stronger if parents see eye-to-eye on the choice of a school. Here's a case in point: A teacher told me, "The father had never seen the place. He came in one day, took a look around, and for some reason decided he didn't like it. They yanked the child out the next week. It's a shame. That boy was happy here. They should have made the original decision together."

TALKING WITH THE DIRECTOR

You and the director of the school should start off by being frank and open with each other. You need to ask about anything that's important to you, including the issues we have just mentioned. He or she needs to know enough about you, your child, and your family to help you make your choice. It is especially important that you and the director share thoughts about the program and about anything else that might impact on your child's preschool experience. Start with your living arrangements. You might say, "I am recently widowed," or "I have a live-in boyfriend who will often be picking Tanya up," or "Sandy has a new stepfather and stepsister," or "Jason has a hearing problem, which we're in the midst of checking into." You will also want to discuss any special dietary or religious requirements, or the fact that you feel strongly about exercise or trips or whatever. Now's the time to air these topics or similar ones.

The director should respond to your information with candor and professionalism. She should also share with you the preschool program's approach to education in as detailed a manner as possible. Some of the other things she should make clear are

- Your financial obligations
- All the school rules and regulations if they're not covered in a handout
- Parent participation—whether you'll be required to participate in the running of the school by fundraising or by donating time or sitting on a committee

THE FIRST VISIT

Don't take your child with you on this first visit. You'll want to be free to talk without shushing your youngster or having to monitor what you say in front of her. Allow enough time to observe in the classroom, tour the facility, and talk in depth with the director. Figure on spending

71

about an hour and, if you can, schedule your visit for the middle of the morning.

First impressions are valuable. Pay attention to what your eyes and ears tell you when you walk into a preschool. You'll get an immediate sense of a general atmosphere. Is it bright, clean, airy, relaxed, cheerful, reasonable, quiet? Does it seem as if the youngsters are enjoying themselves? Although the setting may be somewhat noisy and exuberant, do you get a clear sense that adults are in charge? Are there toys and supplies in evidence and are they in good condition? Is everything *too* neat, *too* sterile, *too* quiet? Are there children crying or wandering aimlessly, looking bored or unhappy? Are there children fighting, or playing in a dangerous way? Do the adults seem to be enjoying the children and interacting with them, or simply keeping them in line?

You don't need to be a child care expert to pick up on these things in the first few minutes. And, of course, pay particular attention to the behavior of the director and the teachers. How are they with the youngsters? Remember, they are the ones who set the tone of the place.

After you've been there a while, you'll begin to get a sense of the rhythm of the day. You'll begin to pick up on certain things, like what the teacher does when a child cries or has to go to the bathroom or hits another child. You'll notice whether independence is valued in the school and whether children are being asked to master things they're capable of doing. You'll see whether the teacher is sensitive to individual needs or is doing activities that some kids can't handle.

Taking everything into consideration, is this a place you would feel good about leaving your youngster?

▲ ■ ●

THINGS TO WATCH FOR

Is there plenty of space for exercise and movement, such as dancing?

Are there climbing and other toys that exercise big muscles?

Is there an outdoor play area or a nearby park?

Is there good indoor and outdoor play equipment?

Is there adequate light and ventilation?

Is there a separate area or room for each age group?

Are there comfortable child-sized tables and chairs? Cubbies for clothing? Nap- or rest-time equipment?

Are things at a child's eye level?

Are toys and other relevant materials accessible to kids, or are they stored on high shelves so that they can only be used with an adult's permission?

Are there designated areas for various activities—for example, a quiet corner, a housekeeping corner, a dress-up area?

Are a variety of materials available?

Blocks, books, clay, trucks, climbing equipment, puzzles, Legos, paints, sand, water, dress-up clothes, a pet corner, and a housekeeping corner are all standard for a well-equipped preschool. However, one or two missing items shouldn't necessarily turn you away from a school that feels right to you on every other count. In fact, it's not as important what kind of materials the center has as it is how they are being used. Some centers have state-of-the-art equipment but it's used in a very formal way, under tight teacher control.

Look for signs of ongoing activity—charts, artwork, block projects, classroom notes, children's dictated stories, and teachers working and talking with groups of kids. Ask about field trips as well as about *regular* outdoor activity.

What the children do—with and without teacher help—is probably more significant than the materials and hardware in the place. Look at memos to parents and other information posted around.

Check the fire-safety provisions. Make sure there are enough exits and that a child can get to them readily. Is there a sprinkler system? Are there extinguishers? We think this is an often neglected and very important area to investigate. Ask about fire precautions, including inspections. And what about security? How easy is it for children to get in and out of the building unobserved? Can strangers wander in?

What provisions are made for caring for and/or isolating sick children? Is there a nurse on staff and are doctors' numbers readily available? What are the procedures when a child is ill? What are the rules about keeping a child home or sending a child home? Is a medical exam or immunization required?

Do the equipment and room layout seem safe (no rugs to trip over, stairs to fall down, bookcases to tip over)? How are the sanitary arrangements? Are the bathrooms clean and easy to get to? Are there enough stalls? Enough sinks?

If food is prepared on the premises, are the stoves and other equipment removed from the traffic pattern of the kids? What kind of food is served and is it prepared in a clean environment? Ask, "Is your food preparation monitored by USDA?"

THE SECOND VISIT

If you like everything you see and hear, you'll want to make a second visit. This time you should bring your child (and your spouse if he or she didn't come the first time). See how your child takes to the place and the teachers. See how the teachers are with your child. Explain to your child beforehand where she is going. But try not to make it seem like a test. Often parents think about the interview this way, and even if they don't say it, the child picks up on the parents' nervousness. If it turns out that the school does want to test your youngster, you may have to decide whether you want to permit testing (see "Testing," page 221).

Usually the director will spend a few minutes talking with your child in a friendly and welcoming way. Then she may suggest that the child join the group while you and she talk. She will reassure the child that you will be right there and that he can rejoin you at any time. Even with this reassurance, a younger child may cling or cry or be frightened. The director will not be concerned about this behavior. You shouldn't be either. Some children have a little more trouble entering a new group or situation than others. Don't necessarily base your decision about a pre-school on how a two-and-a-half-year-old acts on a visit. If this is a spring visit, don't forget that he will be an older and more mature person by the time he enters preschool. So what he does and says now isn't the whole story of how he'll adjust to the group later.

A fuller look at the *program* is in order on the second visit. This would be the time to pay close attention to what the children are *doing,* including playground time, lunch-time, and Circle Time, when traditionally teacher and children get together in a group. Listen to the *talk.* Watch the social groups. Try to get a sense of the level of play, of tension, of cooperation, of discipline.

▲ ■ ●

PHASE-IN POLICY

There are some important concerns to discuss with the director and/or teachers in the school on this second visit. High on your list should be the questions of separation. Separation is the process young children need to go through in order to be able to leave their loved ones comfortably and to be away from them for a while. For most young children it's a big step leaving a parent or other caregiver to start nursery or other preschool. It's crucial for a youngster to master separation in order to have a successful preschool experience. Good preschools recognize this and have devised ways of easing separation (see chapter 5).

Ask if the school has a policy of visiting a child at home. You want a home visit preferably before the child starts school. It can be brief and should happen after your youngster has met the teacher in the center and has spent a little time there, with you on the sidelines. The home visit by the teacher is usually both casual and informal, but it serves several important purposes. It gives you and the teacher a chance to get to know each other a little bit. It gives the teacher a sense of what your family style is so that she can better understand your youngster. And the home visit says to a child that home and school are somehow linked and that the teacher can become part of his extended family. This is the beginning of the partnership.

The other separate piece of the home visit is the school's phase-in policy. Ask how the school handles the first period of adjustment for parent and child. Even if your child has been in a child care center before, he or she may feel some anxiety or shyness with new people in a new place. You may also feel a little anxious in this new situation. You want to make sure that the preschool you pick deals compassionately with the major issue of separation. You really don't want a place that expects you and your child to "tough it out" during those first days or weeks. You want a place where you can stay, or leave and come back, where your child can be for shorter or longer periods (see page 122).

DISCIPLINE POLICY

Another issue you need to get right up front is discipline. Children learn discipline, which is, after all, self-control, by being given a few clear, consistent, and fair rules; by learning constructively from their mistakes; and by being redirected to more acceptable behavior. A child whose parents believe in working toward self-disclipline this way is apt to be pretty confused and unhappy in a preschool with a "bad" corner and/or a teacher who yells and punishes. There's no reason for a good, well-run preschool to have to invoke harsh measures. A good teacher should be able to keep a group of three-, four-, and five-year-olds under reasonable control without yelling, shoving, grabbing, or humiliating, verbally or any other way. In fact, a good teacher knows that these methods don't work. As a parent, you want to make sure that the preschool won't do any of the above to your child or to *any* youngster in the group. Remember that it's sometimes as frightening for a child to see another child being punished as it is for him to suffer it himself.

Matters of discipline are so vital that it's worth asking a few separate questions of the director: What does she think are important discipline guidelines for children your child's age? If the list makes you feel uneasy, or if you see harsh discipline in action, don't hesitate to bring the interview to an end and look elsewhere (see chapter 7 for a fuller discussion of discipline on a day-to-day basis).

SIGNING UP

If all goes well on this second visit, you may want to sign up. Make sure before you do that everything is clear to you —costs, hours, parent responsibilities or obligations. You don't want any last-minute surprises. It may be helpful for you to take a look at the "Portraits of Six Preschools" and at the "Preschool Checklists" at the end of this chapter. Before you put down your check, you may want to make that third visit—unannounced—so that you can see the school briefly when no one is expecting you. You can drop by at the time you bring your completed forms or when you bring your check. It will give you another view, and a useful one.

One last caution: Some parents sign their children up for a preschool that might not otherwise be their first choice, because they feel it will ensure their child a place in the private elementary school of which it is a part. Not all good private schools have equally good preschools. Nor do they necessarily give priority to graduates of their preschool. We think it makes sense to judge the preschool on its own merits rather than looking at the elementary school that will follow.

OTHER OPTIONS

Suppose you can't find a setting in your area that comes close to what you think preschool should be. What are your alternatives as a parent?

Should you keep your child home for a year and hope for things to change? You could do that, if you're not working. Or you could simply get together with a few mothers and fathers and start an informal play group that meets a few times a week, with one or more of you sharing the care. Sometimes these informal arrangements work very well. I know one that went on for a few years and finally grew into a full-fledged preschool. I know others that have broken down because people weren't sufficiently committed to them. For instance, if parents start switching days, pretty soon you've got an arrangement that only the phone company profits by. Another aspect of nonprofessional preschool is that you have to look at it in some ways as if it were professional. You have to ask yourself a few hard questions, such as: Is the neighbor with whom I'm going to share this play group the sort of person I want to be with my child? Is it safe in my neighbor's house? And certainly: How will my youngster like this arrangement? Starting your own play group is a viable alternative to preschool. But unless the participants are professional educators and the place has the proper equipment, you can't consider it the same.

What about starting your own preschool? Without being discouraging, it is probably not practical for most parents to try to set up a professional preschool, although it has been done. It takes a lot of effort to start a nursery school or child care center. There's the hiring of teachers, finding a place, making your way through the licensing regulations. All of this takes months, if not years. If you were thinking of the setting for your own boy or girl, you'd have to be willing to start planning at about the same time as that pregnant mother started looking in the marketplace for preschool. Even then, it's more likely that your second child would reap the benefits than your first. The employee who was the moving force behind the Phelps Child Care Center, for instance, moved away long before the place opened its doors.

Nevertheless, I do know parents who have started the preschool ball rolling. A good way is to go through your own employer, through another local employer, or through a nearby college or university, rather than strike out entirely on your own. That way you'll have a partial source of funding and possibly a site as well. If you are willing to broaden the concept of preschool and get into across-the-board child care, you'll have a bigger pool of potential users who will support the idea. Then, if you can find a professional (a teacher-administrator with early childhood experience), and an architect or interior designer with experience in designing physical space for child care, you can begin to pull things together. Some employers are beginning to realize that it's cheaper for them to subsidize various kinds of child care than to pay for employee absences and inefficiency. To go back to the example of the Phelps Child Care Center (pages 92–96), Phelps Memorial Hospital realized that it could attract more nurses from a greater geographical circle if it could assure them that when they commuted to work they would have child care.

It's up to you as a parent to show your employer or school that your interests, the interests of your child, and their interests all overlap on the issue of child care. Get together with other parents and press for comprehensive child care, with part-time or full-time preschool one of the strands.

If you have your heart set on a Montessori education for your youngster, you might get together with some like-minded parents and contact:

American Montessori Society
150 Fifth Avenue
New York, New York 10011

American Montessori is the largest national Montessori group; it represents 750 schools and can give you help with many aspects of setting up a local Montessori preschool.

The other approach is to enroll your child in the existing preschool that is closest to your ideal and work to make it better. Keep in mind the criteria we've suggested as important. If you have to compromise, be sure it's not on important issues, but on things that you can foresee changing. Then, if you feel the school is deficient in ways that can be remedied, make your concerns known to the staff, director, and other parents at parent meetings after you are an insider. Become active in the school's parent organization and raise questions and offer solutions to what you think are problems, whether it's lack of outdoor play space, too-rapid staff turnover, or anything else you think needs fixing.

A FINAL WORD ON CHOOSING

If you can't get everything you want in a preschool, these are the things we suggest concentrating on:

▲ A director who has early childhood credentials and teachers who have training in preschool education, or equivalent on-the-job experience
• A physical plant that is clean and safe
▪ Group size that is appropriate for your child's age group

If these things are in place, many others will follow. Whatever does not, while not unimportant, can probably be managed.

If you aren't sure what to do about preschool, and you have flexibility, then we say keep your youngster at home for the first three years. There's no evidence that socializing and learning in the preschool setting is better for an under-three-year-old than developing close ties to home, family, one or two significant other adults, and a few friends of the same age.

PORTRAITS OF SIX PRESCHOOLS

A MONTESSORI SCHOOL

Montessori teachers believe firmly in *process* and in children learning at their own rate. "Empowering kids" is the way Marlene Barron, director of West Side Montessori in New York City, describes it. The school has a strong belief in looking at the total child within the family and within the group.

This means that Montessori, too, stresses the parent-child-school triad; parent programs are a vital part of its curriculum. Because the emphasis is on the individual, they don't group children by age in Montessori schools. Recently at West Side Montessori we saw three-, four-, and five-year-olds playing and learning together. Individual attention within a group or community of students allows youngsters to make the most of peer interchange, which Maria Montessori believed was an important way in which children learn. At the same time, because individualized teaching style is matched to learning style, no two children get exactly the same experience. One teacher said, "At Montessori we can give attention to the 'space cadets' as well as to those who are well organized."

There are several things I liked and think worth mentioning about this particular setting. The facility was extremely well equipped and attractive. The rooms were full of light and air; the physical space was beautifully proportioned; the kitchen was a model of utilitarian design. The children were doing interesting things and looked as if they were enjoying doing them. There were several male teachers—an idea whose time is long overdue. Certainly young children should have a chance to see that both nurturing and learning can come from males.

This Montessori preschool takes children for half days (morning or afternoon), 9:00–3:00, or 8:30–5:30. There is an outdoor playroof and lots of Montessori equipment. My sense is that there's tremendous variation among Montessori schools. If I were sending my child to a Montessori school, I'd need to see the school several times.

The Montessori movement is international. There are Montessori schools on every continent as well as in most states of the United States. If you can't find one, you may be able to start one, with the help of the Montessori Association, the professional Montessori group (see page 80). In fact, in our country, Montessori schools have almost always been "parent driven"—that is, the schools have usually been started because parents in a certain community felt the need to have a Montessori setting for their children. Montessori adherents see their approach to education as a force in the lives of parents as well as children, which certainly squares with the theme of this book.

One thing more of interest: A Montessori education does not necessarily end at the end of preschool. Some communities (Houston, Texas, is one) have public elementary and secondary schools based on Montessori methods and staffed by Montessori-trained teachers.

If you're thinking about a Montessori school for your youngster, make sure you are choosing the specific school, not the name alone. Montessori schools do vary, and some schools use the name without the educational backup. A good first question to ask is, "Is this school affiliated with a national Montessori group?"

BANK STREET—A LAB SCHOOL

There are about 124 preschoolers ages three to five in the Lower School of the Bank Street Children's School. Most of them stay until 3:30, but four- and five-year-olds may participate in an afterschool program. All the children get the benefits that come from being in a "lab school" attached to this College of Education. They very often have an additional assistant teacher who's a graduate in the Bank Street Graduate Program. All the teachers here are early childhood specialists and, as a result, the children get a rich diet of learning experiences.

In the Bank Street preschool the children are more or less separated by age group, but often play together outdoors on the rooftop playground. The setup of the rooms gives some idea of the thought that goes into making these settings age-appropriate learning centers. In the threes' room, for example, there's a recipe on the board for making playdough. In the fours' room, there's a recipe for pumpkin cake. This may seem like casual coincidence, but, in fact, there's a carefully-thought-out educational pattern here. Recipes teach children a sequence of steps. These particular choices of recipes are geared to match three- and four-year-old capabilities.

The morning I visited, the fours were having a birthday party for a girl who had just turned five. Her mother had brought in a cake, and the class was sharing it. Teacher Anne Heaney assured me that they would run around afterward and get hungry for lunch. She was aware that this party violated the tenet about snacking on sweets between meals. On the other hand, she felt that this was an "event," and as such it merited a bending of the rules. I thought it a good example of developmental interaction. In this case, the birthday became the learning experience, and at least part of the morning's activities derived from it.

The atmosphere in the room was pleasurably relaxed and casual. On the other hand, I noticed that certain routines were quietly insisted upon. Everyone washed their hands before they sat down at the table. Children sat at small tables in groups of four; no one ran around or was disruptive. *The teachers encouraged talk about everything, including the cake.*

"What kind of cake is this?"

"I see strawberry."

"That green is kiwi."

Most people ate with enjoyment, but one or two youngsters balked at the unfamiliar (to them) fruit. No one urged them to eat the exotic cake. The teachers unobtrusively made the most of the learning opportunities. One youngster was assigned to check off the names of the people who were attending the party from a list permanently tacked on the wall. The five-year-old read the names with no difficulty, while a Hispanic teacher led the kids in singing "Happy Birthday" in both Spanish and English.

One little discipline problem came up during the snack time and was disposed of neatly. A child said, "Anne, Mark is saying *doo-doo* again."

I waited to see if the teacher would make an issue of the bad language, and so did the children. But she simply said quietly to Mark, "Don't say that while you're eating." Clearly, that seemed to lay down a rule and still give Mark an option. All parties seemed satisfied, and there was no more bathroom talk, either while the children were eating or afterward.

Bank Street preschoolers have daily outdoor play as part of their program. They also go to class with a special movement teacher a few times a week. This is in line with Bank Street's conviction that exercise and physical movement are important and that young children learn through their bodies and through movement as well as through their senses and intellect. Kids are encouraged to use their bodies to explore spaces and to practice skills. In this sense

Bank Street School children learn through movement as well as through the senses and the intellect.

it's part of the program rather than an ''extra'' here—movement, song, art, science, premath, and prereading are all brought together as part of every child's general developmental needs and are all offered in an informal way.

Preschoolers are not tested at Bank Street, either before they enter or during the time they're there. The teachers feel, and rightly so, that their observations of a child are closer to the mark than a standardized test would be. This is at variance with the practice in some comparably prestigious private preschools. Many "graduates" of the Bank Street preschool go on to its Children's School, which goes up to the eighth grade. Others leave and go to the public school or to other private schools in the city.

Since the child-parent-school partnership is a basic part of Bank Street College's educational philosophy, it follows that the Children's School operates on those principles. Parents are involved in every aspect of the college as well as of the Children's School. Parents serve on the board of trustees and take their turns at the phone for fundraising events. Above all, they are interested in and involved in the education of their children. At the same time, Bank Street preschoolers are encouraged early on to participate in school activities that involve their parents and teachers and the adult Bank Street community.

A KINDERCARE CENTER

Kindercare is probably the largest chain of providers of preschool/infant/day/afterschool care. It tends about 100,000 children on a profit-making basis from 6:30 A.M. to 6:00 P.M. five days a week and provides them with two meals and two snacks. When Kindercare preschoolers get old enough to attend public kindergarten for a half day, they can be picked up by a Kindercare bus and brought to Kindercare for the other half day. This is a terrific service to working parents. Still, the idea of mass child care takes some getting used to, even if you believe in the principle. Some "kinder" have been in the Kindercare system since they were infants; they're now high school age.

What the net effect of long-term Kindercare preschool is we still don't know. One thing that may be positive is the consistency. All Kindercare centers look essentially alike. They all have manipulative and discovery areas. They all offer a structured preschool language program and a pre-K reading program. The activities and philosophy are the same. Reading and other materials are dispensed from a central location. While this tends to cut down on spontaneity and flexibility and push Kindercare centers toward a B model, it has its positive side. If a family moves a lot, Kindercare can provide an anchor—the same alphabet-patterned rugs, the same nap mats, the same water and sand tables—whether the child is in Virginia or Pennsylvania or Texas.

The outdoor equipment is first-rate. There are slides, swings, climbing and tunneling equipment, and sandboxes. It's all scaled to size, with younger children fenced off from older kids so that the toddlers and twos won't get hurt by the older children. One feature I particularly liked was the outdoor place to ride bikes and toy trucks. On the negative side, I thought some of the teachers at Kindercare far less skillful than others. Teachers of three-, four-, and five-year-olds in Kindercare must have a degree in early childhood, but teachers of toddlers are not required to have one. This may be why I saw two-year-olds sitting for too long and doing crayon-and-paper activities that I felt were far too complicated for them.

On the issue of separation, I was told that the school prefers that parents not hang around. In other words, Kindercare doesn't have a phase-in period, which is part of many nursery programs, including the one at Bank Street. This could be rough on the youngster who needs a little more time to adjust to preschool. On the other hand, we saw no children looking miserable or homesick.

Kindercare centers have three parent conferences a year, as well as family events, such as educational films. They also produce materials for parents that give good parenting information. They have a good rate of retention of kids. Their settings are built on two modules, one that will hold 75 kids, the other 130. The particular center we visited has 85 to 90 children enrolled. Some of them come to Kindercare part-time, like the six- to twelve-year-olds who are part of the afterschool program.

On balance, I found the particular Kindercare center I visited more teacher-directed and less developmentally oriented than an ideal preschool should be. Two-year-olds should not be coloring inside lines, cutting and pasting, or sitting so much. But I also think that the teachers at Kindercare are interested in what parents think, so additional flexibility might be negotiable. I have also heard about Kindercare centers in other states that seem be organized along more developmentally oriented lines. Certainly if you can afford Kindercare and if it's one of the choices where you live, you should take a look for yourself.

A HEAD START CENTER

The Bloomingdale Family Center in New York City is one of the oldest Head Start centers in the country and a fine example of the Head Start model of early childhood education. The criteria for acceptance here are somewhat different from those of other settings:

▲ Income guidelines are adhered to in keeping with federal regulations.

• Preference is given to children with special needs (physically, developmentally, and emotionally handicapped).

▪ Preference is given to former parents who are still income eligible.

▲ Preference is given to families on public assistance.

• Preference is given to families who suffer from unusual stress.

▪ Preference is given to one-parent families.

▲ Preference is given to families from other countries who have recently moved into the neighborhood.

• An accurate reflection of the ethnic makeup of the community is maintained.

Since Head Start is free and you must have a low income to qualify, most of the children who go to Bloomingdale come from poor families. Over 20 percent of the children are handicapped in some way. Many of them have multiple problems; all are considered "high risk" children who need the special attention that Head Start was designed to offer.

Bloomingdale operates on a half-day basis, as do most Head Start centers. The first group gets breakfast, lunch, and snack before being dismissed; the second session gets lunch, snack, and a dinner meal. The basic Head Start program is very much like any good developmental preschool. Children sing songs, listen to stories, play games, work with clay, blocks, and paint, and have outdoor play time. However, there are some differences. One is in the area of social services. Bloomingdale and other Head Start centers all have active parent-education and social strands. Bloomingdale preschoolers and their parents get the benefit of trained social workers, special education teachers, and a consulting psychiatrist who meets with the staff on a regular basis. In addition, director Susan Feingold keeps a file as well as an eye on both present and former students. She and head teacher Marilyn Barnwell are always available if a former parent or a new parent wants to talk.

This particular Head Start center has also initiated a toddler program, which operates for a few hours a day. Youngsters who may have older siblings in the regular Head Start program attend the toddler program with a parent. This helps them get used to the place, so they won't have such a hard time with separation when it's time for them to go to Head Start. It's a sound idea, which other preschools might want to imitate.

The parent-participation part of Head Start is probably one of its strongest points. Each classroom elects two parent "reps," who help make policy and act as spokespersons for the parents. There are frequent parent meetings and several kinds of parent-education programs. Bloomingdale also keeps a videotape record of teachers working with children; these are wonderful educational tools for parents, for special education teachers, and for other professionals interested in preschool.

Head Start as modeled by Bloomingdale is a good preschool setting indeed. It may be the biggest educational bargain around, but there is usually a waiting list. All Head Start centers get funds from the federal government. In addition, a share is supposed to be borne by a local agency. You may find the Head Start center in your town in a church, a public school, or in a community office building.

A COOPERATIVE PRESCHOOL

One type of school that would seem to be ideal in terms of parent partnership is the co-op child care center, as exemplified here by Children's Underground (see chapter 4). Here parents share the costs and some of the administrative and financial decision making of a nonprofit center, and the education director makes the educational decisions. Sometimes parents volunteer as child care aides or help with the maintenance. It sounds great, and often it is if—and this is a big one—it's perfectly clear what you're getting yourself into.

What sometimes happens is that parents don't fully understand their obligations, or they can't fulfill them. The most common complaint about co-ops goes something like this: A parent says, "I'm paying full price on a sliding scale. Why should I have to put in time at the school as well?" Or a parent says, "I'm working full-time, so I can't have the fun of being with my child. Those parents who don't work have the advantage over me, and their kids will get more out of school."

A parent cooperative can be a good way of making preschool affordable and of being a parent partner. Just make sure you know what your responsibilities will be and whether or not you can fulfill them.

A CORPORATE CHILD CARE CENTER

The Phelps Child Care Center is a corporate child care center connected to Phelps Memorial Hospital in Westchester County, New York. It supplies child care, full- or part-time, for Phelps employees and its corporate and community neighbors. It's been in operation less than a year, and right now there's a waiting list in the infant and toddler group, and the preschool is filling up fast.

This corporate center came into being because a group of hospital employees needed child care. In this case the parents' needs and the hospital's meshed particularly well. Nurses are in short supply. The hospital saw a distinct advantage to attracting nurses with families who wanted to work part-time or full-time and wanted professional care for their children that was near their jobs. The employees often commute from long distances. They want child care close to the workplace and care geared to their irregular hours. The Phelps Center satisfies both of these needs and does it in quality style.

The building is on the grounds of the hospital. It's new and handsome, painted in childlike colors, and you get the impression that this design feature was done, as everything else seems to be, for the children rather than for some artificial architectural conceit. Inside, the rooms are equipped with spotlessly clean, practical, child-appropriate furniture and equipment. The preschool rooms have a spacious block corner, housekeeping corner, and loads of easels, as well as neatly kept and accessible puzzles, games, and books. They haven't forgotten much in this place, probably because before the hospital went forward with its plans, it called in consultants who had experience setting up centers for children. It's a one-story building with trees and woods surrounding it and ample play space inside and out. Everything here has been done with thought, and the fact that the parents had a strong hand in it says that it is possible for parents and employers together to make good preschool/child care happen.

Donna Woehrle, the highly experienced and enthusiastic director of the Phelps Center, oversees a staff of part-time and full-time caregivers that is growing with the population of the center. There are two certified teachers in the preschool, both of whom have early childhood training, and several assistant teachers. Some of the part-time staff are students from local colleges who are majoring in education.

Right now the center has a total group size of forty. Of these, thirteen are preschoolers, who can come either part-time or full-time. The center is open from 6:30 in the morning until 7:45 in the evening, so the "full-timers" get a hot breakfast, a hot lunch, and a cold snack in the evening, as well as several snacks during the day. Donna says, "We believe in feeding toddlers and preschoolers, and we find they need a series of small meals rather than three big meals a day."

Most of the parents in the center are first-time parents.

They are all encouraged to drop in during the day, and some do. But just as many moms are content knowing their children are being well cared for, so they don't come by routinely. There's a sign-in procedure for parents when they bring the child in, and a sign-out when they leave. In this way, the center can allow parents more flexibility of time and still keep accurate records of attendance. Every day parents are given a ''report'' of their child's activities.

The day I visited the Phelps Child Care Center, there were seven preschoolers in the group. Since it was a beautiful sunny day, they spent much of the morning outside playing on the swings and slides. They also went for a nature walk with teacher Ann Shea, during which they collected leaves and brought them inside, where they talked about differences in shape and texture. After lunch they had about an hour's rest period. In the afternoon they painted, did puzzles, talked, sang, built with blocks, and read books. There seemed to be no strict plan to the day; most of the activities were ones that the children chose. One of the things they seemed to enjoy doing was playing ''teacher.'' One child would say something like, ''It's Circle Time.'' He would sit on the chair with a book and ''read'' to the others, holding the book face out in a perfect imitation of a teacher. Then another youngster would play ''teacher.'' This game seemed to have great staying power; one or another version of it went on all afternoon.

At one point Ann Shea introduced a new activity: finger painting. I was impressed with the way she helped the children get the most out of this experience without seeming to be giving them a ''lesson.'' She talked about the texture of the paper. (''It's shiny on one side. See if you can tell which is the shiny side.'') She talked about the color of the paint. (''Today we're using a new color— orange. Can you find anything else that's orange around here?'') And she didn't tell them how to paint, she just gave them the general rule. (''You use your fingers.'') That way they were free to experiment, and most of them did. One youngster seemed reluctant to get his hands messy, and no one forced him to participate. He may feel more like it another day.

One of the preschoolers in the group was a handicapped youngster. It was his first day in the Center, and I was curious to see how he would manage and how the other children would behave toward him. Ann had prepared the others for the newcomer's arrival by telling them that he could do many of the things that they could do but that some other things he might need help with. She didn't ask them to feel sorry for him or to treat him differently. She simply suggested that they might want to help him where they could. In fact, Jonathan, who has a form of cerebral palsy, was able to communicate his wants pretty clearly. He got help when he needed it, but not too much was made of his handicap, and the children, after a few minutes of staring, went about their business. Jonathan, for his part, participated in some group activities and ignored others. Once or twice Ann asked a child to help Jonathan reach something or to bring him something, and the child did as asked. I found out afterward that the school really didn't know if this particular bit of mainstreaming was going to work, but as far as I could see, it worked very well. Maybe it was because Jonathan seemed no stranger to a day care setting, but I think a lot of the children's casual, accepting attitude was due the teacher's attitude. It was good for both Jonathan and the other children that they were learning young to live with difference.

Donna Woehrle thinks it's important in a child care center to develop a sense of family. ''Many of these kids don't have siblings,'' she says. ''Children can learn from others both older and younger than themselves." To this end, she has the preschoolers pay frequent supervised visits to the infant and toddler rooms, and for a few of the activities the various age groups come together.

I saw one example of a younger person learning from an older model in the preschool bathroom. One four-year-old boy instructed a three-year-old in how to "aim" standing up. It was a useful and instructive lesson for the younger child.

If you were to try to fit the Phelps Center into one of our three models, it is probably closest to the child-centered or A model. In this case openness of format and child-initiated activity were coming out of deep understanding of Piaget's developmental ideas rather than from failure to develop a more defined program. I also very much got the sense that there was freedom here but never chaos.

The Center would like to set up parenting workshops, but they have not been able to as yet. Donna sees as a continuing struggle the job of maintaining quality trained part-time staff, even though the Center pays its teachers as well as comparable facilities in the area. One of the points she made (and we've mentioned here before) is that staff turnover rate directly affects children—the younger the child, the more likely that new faces will be a source of upset.

The following checklist will be a help to you when you visit preschools. We suggest you make copies and take them with you when you go. Maybe you'll want to refer to it from time to time during your visit and perhaps make some notes or checks immediately afterward.

A Word About Pre-K

Pre-K settings in public schools vary so much that we thought it would be misleading to offer a portrait. However, one excellent pre-K program is described on pages 264–66.

Preschool Checklist

Name of Center or Preschool :_____

Address :_____

Phone Number :_____

Date Visited :_____

Instructions: When you visit a preschool program, take this checklist with you. Place a check mark in the "yes" (y) or "no" (n) column for each item you observe. Compare the results of your checklist for each program you visit to see which program has the greatest number of checks in the "yes" column. In addition, you should be able to answer "yes" to the following questions about the setting that is your final choice :

▲ Do you feel that being in this setting will be a happy experience for your child?

• Do you feel that you will be able to develop a relaxed, sharing relationship with the caregiver?

The Care Providers

Y   N

☐   ☐   If required, is there a current license for operating a child care center conspicuously posted?

☐   ☐   Are there enough adults for the number and ages of children?

☐   ☐   Do the children receive the individual attention,

warmth, and understanding that you would like for your child?

☐ ☐ Are the children happy and playing with each other? Talking to each other? Talking to adults?

☐ ☐ Do caregivers recognize when a child is sad or upset or excited?

☐ ☐ Do caregivers refrain from embarrassing any child?

☐ ☐ Is an effort made to listen to and answer children's questions in ways they can understand?

☐ ☐ Is discipline handled in a positive manner?

☐ ☐ Do adults supervise the children at all times during naptime? If a child does not fall asleep, is the child engaged in a quiet activity?

☐ ☐ Does the caregiver participate in training opportunities in child care/child development?

HEALTH AND SAFETY

Y N

☐ ☐ Is the area for program activities well lit and ventilated?

☐ ☐ Are the indoor and outdoor spaces for children safe and free of hazards? For example: radiators covered; stairways protected; windows protected; electrical outlets covered with safety caps; walkways free of ice and snow; outdoor space fenced and free from debris, broken glass, and so on.

☐ ☐ Are heavy pieces of furniture, such as storage shelves and bookcases, secure and stable so that they cannot tip over?

☐ ☐ Are detergents, household cleaners, and medicines kept in locked storage cabinets?

☐ ☐ Are emergency fire drill and evacuation procedures posted in a conspicuous place in each room and are emergency telephone numbers on each phone?

☐ ☐ Are toys and equipment clean and in good repair (for example, free from sharp edges, splinters, paint chips, and loose parts)?

☐ ☐ Do caregivers get annual physical examinations?

☐ ☐ Is a written health record kept for each child?

☐ ☐ Are there written procedures for securing background checks on new caregivers?

☐ ☐ Are first-aid supplies readily available and does at least one person have a current Red Cross first-aid certificate?

☐ ☐ Does a registered nurse visit at least weekly in programs for children under three years old?

☐ ☐ Is there an adult responsible for receiving children when they arrive each day?

☐ ☐ At the end of the day will your child be released to another person only if you have given written permission for this?

☐ ☐ Are there written procedures to follow when a child becomes sick?

☐ ☐ Is there a clearly written financial policy regarding a child's absence due to sickness or other causes?

☐ ☐ Are the meals and snacks prepared by the caregiver?

ENVIRONMENT

Y   N

☐ ☐ Do the caregivers respect the children's rights to engage in activities by themselves and with other children?

☐ ☐ Is the space arranged so that children can freely select materials according to their own interests and abilities and return them when they have finished?

☐ ☐ Do you hear adults in the program giving praise and encouragement to children to enhance their self-confidence?

☐ ☐ As you see children participating in the program, do they seem to be enjoying the activities?

☐ ☐ Do the caregivers help the children learn from a variety of activities?

☐ ☐ Is the program well supplied with equipment and supplies such as blocks, books, games, toys, and creative art materials?

☐ ☐ Is the space neat, clean, and attractively decorated?

☐ ☐ Is there space for active play and for quiet play?

☐ ☐ Is there a special place away from the busy activities for a sick (or tired) child to rest and yet allow for the caregiver to care for him or her?

☐ ☐ Can children reach the toilet and sink easily and safely?

PARENTS

Y N

☐ ☐ Did the caregiver adequately explain the program to you?

☐ ☐ Did the caregiver ask you about your family's cultural and language background so that activities can be planned that recognize each child's culture?

☐ ☐ Will the caregiver provide you with information

on a regular basis about your child's activities and progress?

☐ ☐ Will opportunities be provided for you to be involved in making decisions about the program and your child's education?

☐ ☐ Were you encouraged to visit and observe the program at any time while your child is participating?

☐ ☐ Does the program give community resource information to parents and invite them to participate in educational activities?

☐ ☐ Is there a copy of the plans for children's daily activities available for parents?

☐ ☐ Will trips to local stores, building sites, parks, library, and so on be adequately supervised? Will your written permission be obtained for each trip?

Adapted, courtesy New York State Department of Social Services.

A TYPICAL PRESCHOOL DAY

What's it like to actually be in a fine, well-run preschool? We spent a morning recently at Children's Underground, a day care center in New York City, which cares for children from two to five years old. The following is a word picture of what we observed and what we thought it meant:

It is 8:00 A.M. on a November morning. Parents and children are beginning to drift in through the big wooden door in the side of the brick church. Some mothers bring their kids. Some fathers are the shepherds. Downstairs in the basement is the preschool day care center. The church houses but is not otherwise involved with its operation. The school is run as a parent cooperative partly financed by the city.

It is a typical preschool in terms of its setup. There are four age groups (twos, threes, fours, and fives). They are separated into distinct "areas" by clever walls of shelves and cupboards. Then there is a large common room, filled with the nursery staples—a block corner, a housekeeping corner, a library corner, easels, sand table, water-play

Block play teaches, among other things, shape, balance, reasoning, and cooperation.

table, and puzzle and game center. There are lots of climbing, active play materials, and a wealth of visual materials, including pictures that the children have obviously cut from magazines and to which they have given titles. There's a children's calendar, a chart of assignments, and a rich assortment of manipulative toys.

There's also an informal breakfast area where a selection of dry cereals, orange juice, milk, bowls, utensils, and paper cups is laid out. About four kids are eating at any one time for the next hour. A few of them don't eat when they come in; they may have had breakfast at home. A few say they have eaten but would like a muffin or juice; they are helped to food or they help themselves. Some parents stay and sit with the children while they're eating. Others leave as soon as the children are settled in. The director eats with the youngsters. So does one teacher.

The teachers move about, getting ready for the day, keeping children company, organizing, supervising, or feeding the guinea pig. As the children finish eating, they get up and begin playing. Since the children are brought to the center at different times, there is free play here from 8:00 to about 10:00 A.M.

One or two children are playing in the sandbox. One child is playing with large plastic Lego blocks. Another is listening to a story. There are dozens of little scenes going on in various parts of the room, and each one has meaning in terms of the many types of learning experiences a good preschool offers. For example:

One father says, "I'm leaving now."

The child doesn't say anything.

The father says, "Do you want me to stay a little longer?"

The child says, "Okay."

The father stays a few more minutes, to make sure the child is comfortable, then leaves.

Another parent has stayed to watch an impromptu puppet show. The child says to the mother, "That's the end of the show. You can go now."

Both these scenes highlight *separation*. In one case it's Daddy who wants to spend a few more minutes watching his daughter. In the second case, the child has learned to be comfortable enough about separating from her mother that she can dismiss her. Separation, as we've already said, is a huge part of the preschool experience and is enacted over and over again in different ways at different times of the day, the week, the month. We notice here affirmation of the claim that sometimes parents have as much trouble separating from the children as the youngsters have separating from the parents. In this setting, the teacher seems very much aware of the separation dynamics being acted out and talks with us about it.

There are about five children still involved with the puppet show. They pass out imaginary popcorn to an imaginary audience. They're having a good time in *fantasy play*. The teacher lets them enjoy it without making any suggestions. A few more seconds of this script and the show is over. The children begin to drift away. The oldest ones hang on the longest, collecting tickets, giving out popcorn, working the puppets for their own amusement. You can almost tell in a preschool room how old a youngster is by how long he stays with an activity. Two- and three-year-olds go from one thing to another in spurts that usually last no longer than ten minutes. But the older children are ready to stay with an activity for fifteen to twenty minutes or more.

Now the youngest preschoolers drift into the "young room" to look at books and to string large pop beads together. The beads are large enough so that they can manage them, yet small enough to help the two- and three-year-olds hone their *fine motor skills*.

Two youngsters decide to play at the water table. They help each other put on aprons before they start. No one tells them to do so. They have learned a useful *routine*; this kind of play requires an apron.

Two other youngsters start to paint. One is three years old. The teacher watches casually as the girl draws a circle with a paintbrush and then fills it in.

The director remarks to us that this is unusual control for a child that age. "One of her parents is a painter," says the other teacher. "Maybe that has something to do with it." The point here is that both teachers and director observe and are involved with the kids; they don't just supervise, they understand, as professionals, just what they're observing. This is a tremendously important aspect of good preschool child care.

Breakfast seems to be over. Some children head toward the block corner. A slight disagreement comes up when a four-year-old breaks up a road-building project started by his peers.

One child says to the teacher, "I don't want her to do that."

The teacher says, "So then tell her you want to finish the road."

The teacher helps the child find the right words, but is gently suggesting that the child use language to express her desires. Again, this is teaching life skills that are tremendously important and will serve this youngster well both in preschool and later on.

In another incident a group of children pass around some little cars, sharing them with one another. One child says, "He has more cars than I do."

The teacher says, "You'll have to talk to the others about it." Here again, the teacher is encouraging children to resolve problems by talking and working them out.

Just then a new family arrives. The mother takes her preschooler to join his group. She leaves a younger toddler standing alone in the room. The other children know this toddler, and the older girls rush over to greet him. They take his hand and shepherd him to the sand table, where they play with him. As they do so, they unconsciously mimic the way their teachers interact with them. Using the teacher as a model, they are learning ways to care for and help younger children.

At about 9:50 the teacher says, ''Time to go back to your area and clean up.'' Even the two- and three-year-olds pick up, and if one of them forgets, another child will remind him. The children are learning *orderliness* and *consistency*. One of the ways they learn it is for teacher and children to clean up together. If the teacher were to pick up for them, the lesson wouldn't stick. If the children were expected to do it all by themselves, it would be too difficult for them at this age.

It is the end of free play time. Everyone who is coming to school should have arrived by now, so the teacher can start group activities without one of the late children missing out. The four-year-olds are toileted and get ready to go to the park for outdoor play with the teacher and aide. This preschool has no playground of its own, so it uses a nearby public park.

While one group goes to the park with its teachers, the remaining two groups go to their ''rooms.'' Children are already outside walking toward the park when a car drives up to drop off four-year-old Steve. With a brief hug, Mom deposits him on the school steps with the teacher and drives off. By the time she reaches the corner, Steve is crying pitiably. Another two minutes and his sobs are uncontrollable. The drop-off has been both too hasty and too late. Steve is obviously totally disoriented. And to top it off, Mom has driven away with the toy truck he had meant to bring to school for show-and-tell.

It takes a while for the director to calm Steve down. She talks with us afterward about the incident. Was Steve a ''problem'' ordinarily? What had set him off? She explains that many four-year-olds can't make the kind of quick transitions that Steve's mom was asking him to make. First, he was late. He knew that. He also knew his friends at preschool were already thoroughly embarked on the morning. He was not going to be a part of that sharing. In addition, he had not had time to say good-bye to his mom in the leisurely way he was used to. That made separation difficult. And finally, he had left his ''piece of home'' in the car. That was the last straw. This four-year-old felt abandoned, and the feeling gave him (and to a lesser extent his teacher) a pretty bad morning.

This is the kind of small daily crisis that professionals are prepared for. Later the director may call Steve's mother to find out what happened and if anything is wrong at home. Clearly, late arrival is hard on everyone.

Back inside with the nonpark group, we notice a homemade poster on the wall. There are pictures of animals cut from magazines. The poster makes a little story, and it is clear that the children have dictated it in response to the question *''How Do They Feel?''*

Picture of tiger: *The tiger feels lonely because he's all by himself in the forest.*

Picture of seal: *The seals feel happy because they're in the water.*

Several other pictures, then on the bottom: *Animals have feelings, too.*

This poster illustrates several things about a good preschool. Both *language* and *reasoning* are being explored. This little exercise was obviously a group effort. Children talked about ideas and came up with explanations of pictures that they thought about. They also had a discussion about feelings that brought them to a conclusion, ''Animals have feelings, too.'' It may not be entirely scientific, but it's sound and useful thinking for this age level. And it's much more likely to keep young Scott or Laura from pulling the cat's tail than the teacher saying "Don't!" or giving a long explanation about not hurting animals.

Now there is a small discussion going on between two children about clothes.

"I got sweat pants. Are those sweat pants?"

"No, they're stretch pants."

"Oh."

We were surprised at the different styles of dress in this preschool. Some children were very dressed up—girls in dresses, fancy shoes, and so on. Other kids wore sweat suits or jeans and sneakers. There was no uniformity of dress and no evidence that children were involved with copying their neighbors' dress. We attribute this to the fact that in this particular center there is great ethnic variety, and there seems to be an easy acceptance of difference, in appearance as well as in cultural styles of dress. The preschool has obviously made an effort to cultivate both *appreciation of difference* and *sense of self*. However, the question of clothing may be more of an issue in some other settings (see "Clothes and Dressing," in chapter 8). The director says that it surfaces from time to time here too.

Now a teacher gets the three-year-olds together for a book discussion. During the time they're sitting in the circle, two boys are annoying each other. The teacher says, in a helpful tone of voice, "John, why don't you move to a different spot?"

Three-year-olds sometimes need this kind of short, simple directive. There was a clear difference between this *conflict resolution* and the one with the four-year-olds. With the threes the teacher didn't suggest that the children talk it over, because they really aren't ready for that. This problem needed a quick, emphatic solution. Simple, direct action is more apt to do the trick with younger children.

The teacher starts talking about the pictures in a book about smell. But the youngsters don't seem to respond to a book about this subject. They are not quite ready for words about smell; they probably would have been more interested if the teacher had some specific items to smell—as Piaget says, "Young children think by doing." The teacher immediately sees that her original idea isn't working; rather than push it, she takes her cue from the children and uses the book another way.

She holds up the open book, so that everyone can see the pictures. "What do you see?" she asks.

A child says, "Look. I see a seagull. It's blue."

Another child says, "The white seagull is bigger. Some of them are very little."

Like typical three-and-a-half-year-olds, these preschoolers are interested in *color, shape,* and *size.* They are in a constant process of sorting out the world, and books and conversation, whether at preschool or at home, help to refine their understanding of these important basic concepts.

The book session is over. The teacher moves to another topic. She says, "Do you know what day it is today?"

A child says, "Wednesday."

The teacher holds up a card with the number 10 on it. She says, "What number is this?"

Nick says, "Ten."

The teacher says, "Okay. Put it up on the board under Wednesday."

From activities like this, the children are beginning to recognize *numbers* and to get an idea of *time.* They have their own homemade calendar, which the teacher helps them to bring up-to-date every day. This also begins to give them a sense of *time* as well as a sense of *numbers* and a first notion of how *records* are kept.

The younger children have come back from outside.

Aides begin to prepare for snack time. Meanwhile the director has been in her office answering calls, but she frequently comes into the room during the morning. There is very little that goes on that she does not see.

The children go to the bathroom before they have a snack. The teacher notices that one of the boys is angry and noisy. She says, "Why are you angry, Abner?"

She keeps an eye on him. She doesn't let him go into the bathroom, as it is crowded right now and his noise would be disruptive. As she heads him off, she says, in a matter-of-fact tone, "Abner, calm down. Then you can go into the bathroom."

Just then a child comes out of a toilet stall. The teacher reminds him, "Joseph, please wash your hands."

The teacher quietly makes sure that routine *health habits* are observed with some consistency. Then she sends the children out to meet another teacher as they finish.

The next group of children will go to the park now. One teacher says, "Paul, I'm glad you decided to go to the bathroom because there are no bathrooms in the park" (a reminder to reinforce the idea of *toilet routines*).

The teacher now says to Abner, who has calmed down and is in the bathroom, "You see, Abner, sometimes there's too much noise in the bathroom and we have to ask someone to go outside." She's explaining why his behavior in the bathroom was unacceptable and why she had to invoke *discipline*.

A child is having trouble with her overalls. Instead of rushing to help her, the teacher helps foster a little *independence*. She says, "You can snap that, Deirdre. Use two hands."

We go back into the common room and sit near a table where the oldest group is painting on clay and talking. One child says, "We like black."

Another one says, "I hate brown."

A third says, "I won't come to your birthday."

His companion says charitably, "Then I'll send you a piece of cake." (Thinks for a minute.) "But it will be crushed."

The third child quickly says, "Then I'll come."

These four- and five-year-olds are having a real conversation. And in this social setting they are gaining experience *reasoning* and *making choices*.

The painting goes on quietly. Some children mix all the colors together and get muddy gray. Others have learned enough about colors, through using them, to keep the colors separate and to control the paint and get it just where they want it.

One child says, "I'm not only using red."

For some reason they are using watercolor paint and it is not covering the clay properly. The children are clearly getting frustrated. Just then the director comes out and sees what they're working with. She says to her aide, "I question the use of watercolor on clay. Use the tempera paint in the jars. It will cover better."

This is the sort of thing that makes for a good preschool —an administrator who not only knows early childhood but who knows *classroom management* so well that she can pick up on something like this.

One other incident happened during the morning that illustrates some of the learning experiences available in a good preschool program. A group of children were busy in the block corner. The first child said, "We have to build Manhattan Island, New York City, the World Trade Center, and the Empire State Building."

The second child said, "We need to build a ramp. To walk up. Right?"

The third child said, "There's more blocks for the roof. Right?"

The fourth child said, "Where should we put the Pound Puppy?"

We noted the other children's reactions. A few of them were clearly puzzled by some of the words used by their peers, such as *World Trade Center* and *ramp*. But as they talked with one another, they began not only to accept the new words but to use them in their proper context. By talking with one another, each child was enlarging his own *vocabulary* and that of his playmates. In fact, we noticed this over and over again. At lunch, for example, there was much discussion about food. One child offered the information that what they were eating was *spaghetti*. Another child said that it was *pasta*. The teacher assured them that they were both right.

By noon everyone has had a full morning. All the groups have been outside to the nearby park, where they have had outdoor physical *exercise* on the swings and slides. When they come back, they have a hot lunch of spaghetti and meatballs, salad, French bread, milk, and a simple fruit dessert. Then cots are taken down from a storage loft and the children go off to nap or rest. Many of them actually go to sleep.

They wake up about 3:00 P.M. Those who don't are gently wakened at 3:30. "Waking up is a big transition," the director said. "Teachers are there for younger children especially, who may be disoriented and need extra help in toileting and/or dressing."

After a brief group time of songs, stories, or sharing, the children go to play outside again. When they come back, they play quietly with table toys or games or they look at books. One by one they are picked up to go home.

During the darker days of winter, they will often forgo the second park trip and play indoors in the afternoon. Special activities—collage, clay, or other art projects or running games inside occupy the afternoons and are carefully planned to be open-ended so that those children whose parents pick them up a little earlier won't feel they're missing a lot.

We made an interesting discovery during our day of observation. The preschool programs that *seem* so seamless and casual have a great deal of work and planning behind them. Teachers, director, aides, cook—everyone in the school—worked to make that day a rich experience for the children. And they do it every day. And obviously every day is different.

The most exciting thing about visiting any developmentally oriented Type C preschool is the realization of how many academic skills are embedded in the program— and learned in a much more meaningful way than if they had been formally taught to these three-, four-, and five-year-olds. If you have any doubt that children get plenty of premath and prereading instruction through play activities geared to their interests, let's just do a rundown of what can come out of a typical day.

A great deal of counting and number activity comes up. For example, a class trip to the store to get fruit for lunch becomes a chance to begin to understand money. Measuring to make a recipe requires practice in understanding quantity. And then—How many days until Friday? How many pieces of puzzle? How many blocks do you have? How long is my foot? How many days of rain did we have last month? How many pieces of apple for you, how many for me? If I eat two, how many do I have left? How many people are here in school today? Then how many are absent? How many triangles make a square? How many nickels make a dime? Or—Let's see what happens when we put one half cup and then another half cup into the cup measure.

These are not just idle exercises. They are useful queries that children come up with and that teachers facilitate in the course of children's preschool play. They are also basic mathematical concepts that form the crucial base data for math learning.

The same thing is true of language and prereading skills. I was struck by the many rich language activities that took place in the good preschools I visited. Instead of seeing children with their faces screwed up and pencils clutched in their fingers struggling over word sheets, I saw youngsters listening to stories, expanding their own vocabularies in dictated stories to the teacher, "reading" their own names and the names of their friends, printing classroom lists and posters with invented spellings, beginning to decode familiar words posted over shelves, and being encouraged by teachers to explore letters, signs, and every other aspect of language. The social and other abstract thinking skills that came out of a single typical day point up the riches embedded in good preschool.

And the social aspect is the cement that pulls the academic or cognitive strands together. Indeed, social skills make learning possible. Some public schools are aware of this fact. That's why social maturity is often one of the criteria for kindergarten entry. Skills such as waiting your turn, sharing, listening to directions, concentrating on a task, getting along with other children, working in a group, expressing your opinion, redirecting anger, reasoning, and being independent and are all vital to later school life.

The fact that both the cognitive and the affective content of the foregoing typical preschool day were cast in a playful mode in no way negates their importance. On the contrary, it makes them that much more powerful. Parents (and educators too) sometimes fall into the trap of thinking that in order for kids to learn, there ought to be at least a little formal ''teaching'' and some evidence of struggle. So it may seem that young children can better learn premath and prereading and other academic skills by working hard writing in workbooks for the reward of a star. Certainly it's a tangible thing for a three- or four-year-old to bring home written work. But the truth is that in terms of learning, the star may be the only thing that sticks. Young children don't retain much of what they learn by rote. What really stays with them and what they can build on are real-world activities geared to their capabilities.

You may want to go and spend a similar morning or afternoon in a good preschool sometime. We recommend it as a learning experience, even if your child doesn't go there. It's educational to watch the pros at work, and you can't help but come away with a clearer idea of what good preschool is all about.

THE FIRST DAYS: SEPARATION

There goes Maggie, hand in hand with Mom. They're off to Maggie's first day of preschool. Maggie is wearing a brand-new bookpack and a cheerful expression. Mom is smiling with eager anticipation. What's wrong with this picture? Nothing. Except that it isn't typical. In real life, more often than not, both Mom and/or Dad and Maggie go off to school with mixed feelings. Their expressions are better described as pensive, even worried. In a true-life scenario Maggie, her parent, and the preschool teacher all are dealing with complex sets of emotions. Let's look inside the heads of Maggie and parent for a minute and imagine what is really going on.

The parent may be thinking: I'm about to lose my little girl. Why did I decide to do this? I wonder if I'm making a mistake. I'm going to miss her so much. Will she be all right here? I've heard so many stories about child care centers. Will she do well? I hope the teachers will like her. I remember *my* first day of school, how scared I was. Come to think of it, I was older. I'll bet Maggie is scared too. She doesn't show it. But she *did* wet the bed last night. She hasn't done that in a while. She's got that ugly old toy dog with her. She insisted on bringing it. I hope the teachers don't make her give it up. If they do, she'll cry. I'd better talk to them about it. Will they resent that? I'm glad this preschool has a transition time for the first few weeks.

The child may be thinking: Why do I have to leave home and Mom and Dad? Who are all these strange children? Some of them look different from me. Will that teacher know how to take care of me? What if my mom goes away and doesn't come back? I DON'T KNOW HOW TO GET HOME. Is my mother going to leave me in this strange place? Maybe if I cry, she'll stay with me. What if I have to go to the bathroom?

The teacher may be thinking: So many new children to get to know. There are a lot of criers this year. Kevin's acting awfully wild. Hope he'll settle down after we get to know each other. Here comes another parent wanting to talk. I wish she didn't want to have a conference now, when I have my hands full. But I don't want to be rude, and what she has to say may be important for the child. I hope the new teacher we hired will work out. Maybe this group will be as special as last year's. Too bad I didn't get to spend more time with that little Maggie before school opened, I think it would have made it easier for her. She looks terrified! It's good that her mother arranged to stay for the transition week. I know it was hard for her to get time off, but it's important for Maggie.

These are only a few of the thoughts that may go through the heads of parents, children, and teachers. During the first days of preschool, everyone has multiple feelings. Children are often under a certain amount of stress, even if they don't show it. Parents may feel guilt, even if the need to work is not what drove the decision to enter a child in preschool. Some parents feel guilt at feeling liberated by having a child in preschool. Teachers worry over whether they'll be able to cope with a new job or more kids or changes in routine. But of all the emotions that erupt during these first days, the most pervasive is the trauma of *separation* felt by parents and children.

WHAT SEPARATION IS AND WHAT IT MEANS

If the first job of the three-way partnership is choosing the right preschool, certainly the second one is to cope with the many feelings of all three members when preschool starts. Dr. Nancy Balaban, in her book *Learning to Say Goodbye,* shows the complex nature of the bond between parents and children that makes for the painful feelings when separation comes. She points out how powerful these feelings are and how they recur at different times in a child's life and are remembered by parents from their own childhood.

What is that special glue that bonds us to our kinfolk? Why does it seem to be so much more difficult for some children to tug loose than for others? Separation seems to be a process that goes on throughout our lives. First, the baby separates physically from his mother. Later he becomes reattached to her and to his other parent or other person who provides him with his basic needs. Still later he develops a basic trust in a few significant other people in his life. These *attachment* feelings are vital to his life and are the emotional framework of loving and caring that he will build on. The other side of the attachment coin is separation. The baby gives up the breast or the bottle for a cup. The toddler gives up a worn-out blanket. He learns to separate from Dad or Mom or both of them for a certain number of hours a day.

At one stage and another he seems to have attachment and separation sorted out. He is able to both let go and cleave to a loved one. But it is not easy to learn two momentous life lessons—separation and attachment—all at once, particularly if people can't explain things to you in terms you can understand. So, young children seesaw back and forth between being able to tolerate separation and being miserable about it. Imagine a two-year-old's puzzlement when a parent says, "I'll be right back," as he closes the door of the car and leaves the child with someone the child has just met. What does *right back* mean? Who is this person? Two minutes may seem like two hours to a little person whose parent has disappeared through the dark doorway of a store. It is precisely because a two-year-old now has a deeper understanding of what her parent means to her that she feels so bereft when her parent leaves. Yet when she's three or three and a half, she may enter a new stage where she is able to handle separation more gracefully, with help from her parents and teacher. Each time a child successfully crosses one of the separation hurdles, she takes a giant step toward maturity.

Entering preschool is one of the times when the trauma-drama of separation will be most likely to show up. It has nothing to do with how good a parent you have been or even with whether your youngster has been in child care before. It does have something to do with your child's age/ stage. (For example, two-year-old children will generally have more trouble with separation in nursery school than threes and fours.)

But it depends on the child, too. I have one son who had a great deal of trouble with separation. When he was two and three, he couldn't even bear to give up long pants for short ones when the seasons changed. My other son had much less trouble. It could have been differences in my behavior or my husband's, or differences that stemmed from the children's birth order. More likely, it was that they were and are two distinct personalities, so they handled separation and attachment in distinctly different ways. Knowing your child, you may be able to gauge pretty accurately how she or he will act upon being separated from you.

Separation blues are not confined only to children. Parents feel them too. Mothers and fathers may have a hard time seeing those chubby little legs climbing up the steps of the little red preschool for the first time. In this parting a parent may feel sadness and nostalgia, as if it were the end of an era. And for some parents, taking a child to preschool may stir up unhappy memories of forced separation or harsh teachers in their own childhood.

Common as these feelings are, it is important that mothers and fathers come to terms with them and try not to let them rub off onto their kids. The "separation blues" are catching, and if your child senses that you have reservations, she's more likely to have them too. Good preschools know and understand how parents feel. That is why phase-in time is a part of all good preschool programs. It is designed to help both parents and children overcome this first hurdle and start the partnership off on the right foot.

HOW PHASE-IN WORKS

A transition or phase-in to preschool is a series of steps that help a child ease into the preschool routine with a minimum of separation trauma. The first step is usually the visit by the child and parent to the school together. This helps the preschooler to connect a real place with that vague word *school* that he has heard so much about. Next may come a visit by the teacher to his home. This helps him to get the idea that the nursery or center and home are somehow linked. Then comes the actual start of preschool. In most phase-in programs the parent stays the first few days or even few weeks and gradually tapers off when the child seems comfortable enough to stay the full morning or full day in school without Mom or Dad.

Here's the way one well-run child care center handles transition to a full-day program:

Day One: The child stays at the center for one or two hours, with Mom or Dad sitting in.

Day Two: The child stays a little longer and goes to the park in the morning with the group. The parent may or may not go along, depending on how things are going. If the parent does leave, he or she is still nearby and available.

Day Three: The child stays through lunch. The parent is not there but is a phone call away.

Day Four: The child stays through naptime without parent, then goes home.

Day Five: The child stays for a full day without the parent if the parent and school feel she is ready.

The number of days for phase-in needn't be cast in concrete, so long as you and the school agree to a beginning period set aside for the process of separating. Some kids need more time, some can do with less. Older children and/

or veterans of day care or nursery school may be able to be on their own sooner than the five-day plan outlined here. A shy child or a child under three may need two weeks or even three to work up to staying for the full program day, according to Ann-Marie Mott, director of Bank Street's Lower School.

For some parents a leisurely phase-in policy may require special arrangements at the workplace. Sometimes Dad and Mom share phase-in time. But not everyone can manage time off from the office or can leave a younger child at home with a sitter. Parents who can't manipulate their schedules often feel guilty about not being able to follow the preschool's policies on phase-in to the letter. For those parents, a little improvisation may be needed. If you can't be with your child, have Grandma phase in, or a sitter the child knows, or the caregiver.

Can't this phase-in idea be carried too far? One parent I spoke to was a little impatient at the preschool's insistence on a slow transition. Although he liked everything else about the school, this aspect seemed to him a little like coddling. He said he could remember saying a tearful good-bye to his mother at the kindergarten door and being left to fend for himself. "I managed and was okay," he boasted. Another parent said, "My youngster seemed to be ignoring me completely." In fact, even the child who doesn't seem to be having separation problems may really need his parent to be there for a while. He can move about and play freely once he feels tethered by that invisible cord to the person he loves.

Certainly kids have faced a lot more traumatic experiences than starting preschool without a transition. Nevertheless, if we know that separation is a process that children must deal with successfully, why not help the process along? Here's what Mary Hayes, director of the

123

Children's Underground, has to say about the benefits of a phase-in period: "The child has to learn to trust us before he can be free to learn here. Having a parent with him for a while tells the youngster that his parent trusts us and that we're both interested in him and working together for him. He senses the partnership, and after a while he can let his parent go and still feel safe and comfortable."

How Parents Can Help Transition

The first step is to make sure that the school takes separation as seriously as you do. We've already talked about choosing a school that has some sort of phase-in or transition policy and one that supports a home visit or some other time to begin to get to know a youngster before he starts school. But suppose the school doesn't have an official transition policy, although it supports the general idea? Then you'll have to create your own transition time by bringing your child to the school for a few shorter visits when he starts and staying there with him for as much time as is necessary. If you and the teacher work out the schedule together and you're not interfering with some routine, there should be no problem with your visiting.

In my interviews some parents talked about what they thought were arbitrary transition rules. But actually a larger number complained not about transition time but about the lack of it, or about promises of transition time that weren't kept. Several mothers and fathers described being shooed out of a center or being urged to leave a child who was clearly suffering from separation or who wasn't ready to be left.

What should you do if you feel strongly that your child needs you and the teacher is giving you your walking papers? This is probably one of the most touchy and common scenes at the beginning of preschool. And it's important how well you and the preschool can work it out. If it happens during the first few days, you'll simply have to say that you want to stay with your child for a few more days and tell the teacher why. If you put it in terms of her needs ("I want to help you make sure that Tom is comfortable in the group"), it generally works better. You can be cheerful but firm in your resolve. After all, it's your child and your right to be there. The preschool should have no objections. However, sticking around may be especially difficult for the parent who is the last one still sitting on that too-small chair with a child attached to his leg. A teacher may call you aside and say, "Why don't you leave for a little while and we'll take over?" You may have visions of hysterics, but in fact the teacher may just be right.

In this situation try to hear what she has to say. Does she think the child has had enough time to get comfortable in the new setting? What does she plan to do to make the child comfortable when you leave? Does your child always

Both parent and child may experience some pangs at the beginning of school.

have a hard time with change or transition? If so, this maybe a case where you do have to "bite the bullet" and leave, at least for a little while.

The teacher should be able to give you concrete answers to your questions and also to offer some reassurance about the pattern of your child's separation problems, based on her experience. If what she says makes sense, if you have confidence in the setting, and if you've gone through at least a week of phase-in already, you may want to follow her advice. But keep in mind that in the last analysis, it's your child. If you really feel that he needs you, then you will have to pull rank as a parent and insist on staying a little longer.

Spending the time on separation at the beginning of preschool can pay off in terms of everyone involved— child, teacher, and parent. Your child certainly will get more out of preschool after he has coped successfully with leaving home. Children are freer to make friends and to grow in other ways if they have been helped to take this big step toward independence. And you will feel more comfortable knowing that your child is happy and secure in preschool rather than hanging back every morning. As for the teacher, her job will be enhanced by having children who participate fully in what she has to offer.

SOME SEPARATION SCENES

According to preschool educators, almost all children feel some separation and loss feelings when they enter preschool for the first time. But different children handle the feelings in different ways. Here are some separation issues that may come up even after a successful transition.

▲ ■ ●

NAPTIME BLUES

Three-year-old Sarah did fine all morning at the day care center. But around lunchtime she began to get edgy, and by naptime she was in tears. She told her teacher and her parents that she hated naptime and missed her mom "too much." Her teacher understood Sarah's problem; she knew from experience that separation loss can be particularly keen for young children at naptime. It is then that they may be most vulnerable, because they're tired. Also, it may be a time of the day when at home Mom or the caregiver gives them special attention—cuddling or a story. Being one of a group being tucked in just isn't the same.

In this case, Sarah's teacher asked her mother to describe what she did at home. Bringing a comforter from the bed at home, along with the record that was a part of the nap ritual, eased Sarah's naptime.

DELAYED SEPARATION REACTION

One parent-and-teacher team I met had to do real detective work to discover why young Kathy was happy the first week of preschool and distraught the second. In this case it seems that Kathy, who is under three years old, had gotten the wrong message about school. She thought it was a place you went to for a few days, like the vacation at Grandma's a few weeks before. Having gone to preschool for what felt like a long time, she was shocked to find out that it wasn't "over," like the vacation, and that her parents were now going to leave her to go it alone!

It's often hard to figure out what young children make of what we tell them, especially about events that are going to happen in the future. That's why it is always good to be clear about preschool—what it is, what's going to happen

127

there, and when. In this case Kathy's teachers and parents had to get her used to the idea of going to preschool "tomorrow" and "after tomorrow."

Another not-unusual delayed reaction to preschool is typified by this scenario: Tommy, three and a half, made a fine adjustment to preschool. He just skipped right in and made himself at home. All of a sudden, three weeks later, he balked at going and seemed to hate everything about it. Why?

It's hard to say for sure why a youngster may suddenly (and usually temporarily) regress after adjusting to preschool. Sometimes something specific, such as a fight in school or a teacher being absent, can shake up the newfound separation skills. Other times (as in Kathy's case) the novelty of preschool wears off. The realization that preschool is going to be every day can seem like forever to a young child.

Whatever the reasons, it is important for parents to recognize the symptoms and to get together with the teacher as soon as possible in order to get to the bottom of it.

Too Young

Dennis started preschool at two and a half. His parents had talked with him about it, shown him books, brought him in to the school for a trial run. Still, as soon as he walked in the door that first day, he began clinging to his dad. And he stuck to him like glue from then on. It was uphill all the way for Dennis in preschool. In spite of special attention from teacher and a three-week period of adjustment where Mom or Dad stayed with him, Dennis cried steadily whenever he was left. His mother said, "After the teacher and I had both done our best, I asked myself, 'Why does every child have to go to nursery school?' And if I'm doing it for *him,* all I seem to be doing is making him miserable."

So Mom took Dennis out of preschool. Now he's four and a half and has again started preschool half days. This time around he loves it. A little maturity, perhaps, has brought about a new ability to separate from home.

In general, younger children tend to be more troubled by separation than older ones. Mainly it is because they don't yet have a clear mental picture of Mom and Dad when they're not with them. The person who is not there does not exist for a two-year-old. This is pretty scary when it's a parent we're talking about, and it takes some doing to help a two-year-old understand that "out of sight" does not mean "gone forever."

Parents of two-to-three-year-olds starting preschool need to pay particular attention to phase-in time. They can help separation by being willing to stay at the school for at least a week and to continue to drop by during the day if that's possible. Sometimes having a parent come and go for a while helps to set in place the idea that Mom and Dad do come back. Some preschools suggest that a photo of the family be left in the child's cubby during those rough first days. It also helps a two-year-old to be told clearly what is going to happen. A parent may say, "I'm going now, but I'll be back by the time you are ready to eat lunch." But never say it unless it's true.

Sometimes, of course, it's not possible for a parent to get away from work or home to help in this way. Then sensitive teachers will step in and try to provide the attention, cuddling, and comfort that a young child may be missing.

▲ ■ ●

TOO GOOD

Aretha, three years old, is very good at the center. Her dad thinks she's made a good adjustment to preschool and wants to declare the separation period over. No more staying for him. But her teacher has a different take on the situation. Aretha's a little *too* good. Her teachers recognizes this as one of the ways some kids cope with separation. She notes that Aretha spends her day watching the activities that are going on rather than participating in them. She seems to be putting in her time at school waiting for the day to be over rather than enjoying the activities at hand. For Aretha, life begins when school ends. She hasn't quite—yet—separated from home.

A good teacher will pick up on Aretha's behavior and spend some time weaning her away from her intense preoccupation with home. She'll figure out something that Aretha especially enjoys doing and try to engage her. If Mom or Dad can hang around at preschool for a while longer, Aretha may feel freer to play. "Good" children like Aretha still need to use their parents as a kind of home base from which they can move out and explore.

TOO BAD

Some kids respond to separation by turning unruly. They fight or bite, kick or generally turn ornery. This is the other side of the adjustment coin, and it's harder to take than Aretha's passive response. What parent is prepared for separation pangs turning into temper tantrums or aggressive behavior? A good tip-off that it is separation pangs is if your child doesn't act that way at home. But once you have the diagnosis, you will still want a solution. It is maddening to see a decent young citizen suddenly spin out of control. "Why did I start this preschool business?" you may wonder. There is a great temptation when your child turns wild to yank her out of preschool. But a conference with the teacher and/or the director of the preschool will almost certainly clear the air and is likely to set a course that will solve the dilemma. Sometimes time itself will straighten things out. More likely time plus a course of action that acknowledges where the behavior is coming from works best. Somehow it is comforting to know that a child is in a temper because she misses her mom rather than because she is purely a hellion.

BACK TO BABYHOOD

When four-year-old Abdul started school, he seemed to handle separation from his parents well. But then he started to suck his thumb again, something he hadn't done in months. The teacher noticed that the thumbsucking usually began around lunchtime. "I don't want to eat this lunch," he would say, inspecting each item of the menu as if it were a foreign object and acting out his preference for his finger as food.

Some children go back to thumbsucking because they're homesick. Others wet the bed or revert to baby talk or wanting to be fed. These are all variations on the theme of "I can't handle being separated from my loved ones."

Often the teacher will help a child to understand what's going on with his emotions. A teacher will say directly, "I know it's hard for you to say good-bye to Mom and Dad." She can also reach out and try to form the special, reassuring bond that says to the child, "I'm your friend." Both of these actions support the child's right to his feelings while still acknowledging the parents' right to leave. In other words, the answer to a child's acting out of "It's hard for me to leave you'' should never be, ''Don't be a baby.'' Rather it should be help in dealing with his real feelings and coping with separation.

SECURITY BLANKETS

Often a child will have an elaborate ritual involving bringing an object from home to school. Sometimes it's a blanket or a diaper. Sometimes it's a tattered toy animal or a toy truck. Whatever the object, it has some kind of magical power to carry him through the day, and woe to the parent who allows him to forget it. Annoying as the daily search for that object can be, you have to admire the cleverness with which young minds work out this piece of business. *I'm missing home, so I'll bring a little piece of home with me!*

Good preschool teachers have seen a lot of blanket bearers in their time. Eventually the blankets are abandoned, and if it helps a child in the meantime to cart his Linus or whatever, it's best to let it be. If a teacher should complain about having to keep track of the object, point out that it is better for her to have to keep track of a piece of cloth than to deal with an unhappy kid. You shouldn't be defensive about your child's need; thousands of children cart blankets and teddy bears to preschool.

There's another kind of security blanket some youngsters devise. A young child may be unable to cope with his or her new feeling of attachment to someone other than Mom. As a result, there will be a temporary displacement of affection. A preschooler will come home announcing, ''I like my teacher better than you.'' Or ''The cook makes better food than you or Daddy.''

Mom and Dad may feel a bit put out by this fickle behavior, but it doesn't signal any permanent alienation of affection. It simply means that the youngster has worked

out a personal way of separating. Soon she'll learn that
you don't have to have love for parent *or* teacher. You
have enough room in your life for all your loved ones.

SEPARATION AND TIMING

Good timing may not be everything, but in the case of
preschool it is one of the issues that comes up over and over
again. It seems to have a significant effect on preschool
success in general, and on separation in particular.

Here are a few general tips on timing your child's entry
into preschool:

▲ Try to catch an optimum development stage for
starting preschool if possible. Three, for example, is
generally an age of equilibrium. A three-year-old
may be more likely to get off to a good start than a
negative two-and-a-half-year-old.
• Catch the clues your child may be giving you.
Sometimes the best time for launch is when a child
talks a lot about preschool and appears eager to go, or
when a friend of hers is starting. In other words,
when all systems are go.
■ If there's a preschool year or semester, try to start
at the beginning. It's easier for a child if everyone is
new than when she's the newcomer to the group. Even
in preschools that permit enrollment all year, most of
the routine seems to be geared for September entrance.

Start talking about preschool and describing some of
what happens in school before the child goes. How much
before? It depends on the age of the child. Two-year-olds
don't have a strong sense of the future, so they can't en-
compass "next September" or "next month." You can

say, "When you go to school, the leaves will be changing color." Or, "You will go to school when [a sibling] goes."

Remind your boy or girl of the joys he or she can look forward to. "There are lots of books and toys in school." Or, "You can play on the slide in the park every day when you go to school." Or, "You'll make lots of new friends." Whatever is true and will appeal to a child is worthy of discussion. But, for a young child, short talks are best. Don't ask a child over and over whether he wants to go. Whether or not to go to preschool is not a decision that young children are capable of making in advance. If you ask, you may not get yes for an answer.

A visit or visits in advance with the child, separate from your evaluative visits, is a great investment of your time. It establishes your youngster as a full partner in the preschool venture. A good preschool will suggest this and even plan for it. A get-together with class parents and their children before school starts is a dry run that may not only smooth a few of the bumps of separation but set something going parent-to-parent and child-to-child. An adults-only evening meeting of parents and teachers is also a way to get cooperative interaction going. A visit to the home by the teacher before school opens will show a child that teachers and parents are friends. Many teachers feel that they visit as much for the parent as for the child.

Books can help a child to picture what preschool will be like. *My Nursery School* by Harlow Rockwell (Greenwillow) is excellent; so are *Will I Have a Friend?* by Miriam Cohen (Macmillan) and *Going to Day Care* by Fred Rogers (Putnam's).

▲ ■ ●

Preseparation Timing

▲ Keep the home atmosphere relaxed for a day or two before preschool starts. Plan for an orderly entry, with plenty of time allowed for false starts and last-minute stalls. Try not to be rushing home from vacation late the night before school starts or having the painters in that morning.

• Make sure your child knows what to expect. You will have already taken the child to the school, but a gentle recap the day before can smooth the way. You might want to read to your child or sit down for a few minutes and make up your own script about how the day will shape up. Focus on positive things like, "You're going to have a cubby with your name on it." Don't say, "You have to be good and do everything the teacher tells you to do."

▪ During a family crisis, such as a death, divorce, or separation, a child may need to be near her parent or parents. In such a situation it may be better to put off starting preschool for a while and wait until things settle down.

▲ When there's a new baby in the house may be a convenient time for *you* to start an older child in preschool, but it may be hard on the other sibling. Timing entry so that it is either well before the baby comes or after the baby has been around for a while usually works better if you can manage it.

• If a child has been physically ill or has serious emotional or behavior problems, you'll need to share the information with the school. A sympathetic director can often help you make a decision here. In the case of behavior problems, preschool can sometimes be the solution, but not always. Some parents don't like to

135

start their child off in preschool with a problem as part of the record. So they withhold information that the school should know and that will help the child. Never hold back on this sort of thing.

▪ Moving to a new house and/or neighborhood is apt to be hard on young children. Sometimes preschool is a social boost during the adjustment period. Sometimes it isn't. This is one you'll have to play by ear. If your child has been to day care or preschool before the move, it may be better to continue the routine.

▲ Saying good-bye may be hard at both ends of the day. Some children find it hard to separate from preschool when it's over. Johnny may feel that he'll never get to play with the trucks again. Cheryl may hate to leave the tricycle, for fear somehow it won't be there again in the morning. One pair of friends have trouble parting from one another at the center when it's time to go home. Every day when they sense that it's time for their parents to come for them, they run and hide. After their parents have gone through the charade of pretending to look high and low, they pop out of their hiding places, yelling ''Boo!'' This is their way of handling separation.

WHAT PARENTS SHOULD KNOW ABOUT SEPARATION

Separation is a process, not a problem. Still and all, the feelings are powerful. They need to be respected and understood. No parent should be embarrassed if his child does not skip off to school as jauntily as the neighbor's youngster. Children react differently to separation from parents. The child who skips right into the group may show his difficulties with separation later on, or in ways less easily detected.

The important thing for parents to know is that separation and attachment are both major elements of growing up. It is good for children to learn to part from parents and/or significant others without pain and to rejoin them with joy. Preschool can be a good place to enjoy this first taste of independence. Pat Baughman, who teaches in East Stroudsburg, Pennsylvania, and is one of the greeters of kindergarten children each fall, told me that she notices that it's easier for children who have been to preschool to leave their mothers or fathers at the schoolhouse door. She suggests that separation is often easier for them because they have had some practice.

SETTLING IN

After your child has been in preschool for a while, it will begin to feel like old times. The routines of coming to preschool and going home will be second nature. She'll greet the teacher as a friend and maybe start to visit around with other children a little bit after the session, if it's a half day.

Yet, like the other aspects of a child's life, preschool is never altogether static. Children grow. That means change. Change will surface sometimes from week to week (even Friday to Monday!) in a child's relation to school and to the people there. Things learned at home will be brought to school and vice versa. Events at home will affect preschool life, and what happens at preschool will have an impact on home. In this sense, preschool is not simply a matter of one major coping experience—mastering separation. For a young person it also involves mastery of a series of small challenges that come out of daily life at home and at preschool.

Actually, this coping, growing, and adjusting goes on in the parent and teacher corner too. For a teacher, it's getting to know the child individually and in the group and making judgments as to how the program can best serve that child.

Josie could use a little encouragement toward more physical activity.

Ralph is very quiet in Circle Time. What can we do to encourage him to talk more?

Jonna doesn't seem to know how to use many of the manipulatives. She'll need help with that.

And for the parent, it's getting to know the teacher and her personal style, understanding and accommodating to the way you and she communicate. As things come up day-to-day, teachers and parents need continually to fine-tune their understanding of each other in order to make their partnership work.

What are some of the day-to-day issues that are likely to come up in preschool?

DAILY SCHEDULING : THREE POINTS OF VIEW

One of the most common hassles of preschool is scheduling. Most families these days are ruled by the clock. Every minute counts. You plan your time carefully, and it often requires both parents to manage the agenda successfully. Even then you may feel it is only with the most creative juggling that you're able to get everything squeezed into the day. In a recent *Fortune* magazine survey, it was found that mothers and fathers worried about the fact that most of them must ask their children to conform to their own hectic schedules. So it's no wonder that when three-year-old Danny has to get to preschool at a certain time and Mom and Dad have to be somewhere else by that same time, things can get hairy.

The crux of the problem is that grown-ups know about time and how precious it is, and young children simply don't understand it. How do you explain that you have to be out of the apartment in fifteen minutes to someone who doesn't yet know the number 15 and has no sense of what a minute is? That's why when you're down to the wire, you're likely to hear, "But I need to find my teddy bear," or "I didn't kiss my dolls good-bye," or "Where are my sneakers? I need my sneakers today."

One parent said, "I travel thirty miles to work every day and I take my daughter, Ardis, with me and drop her off at a child care center near my office. Each morning is a nightmare. It's almost impossible for me to get her going. We end up with both of us on edge. I'm late for work every day and I can't seem to change the pattern."

Meanwhile the preschool teacher is surely affected by the scheduling bottleneck that gives Ardis's day such a frantic start. While a good preschool doesn't hew to a rigid time frame or give out late slips, the program usually does start around a certain time. One teacher put it this way, "It's more difficult for a teacher to give equal attention to all the children when everyone arrives at a different time. And the program really doesn't work as well for the child when his parent straggles in after the morning's activities are well under way. Once the group forms in the morning, it may be hard for a child who comes in late to insert herself. As a result, she may miss the best parts of that day altogether and disrupt the day for other children." So, in fact, arriving at preschool on time is important for everyone's sake (see chapter 4).

WHAT PARENTS CAN DO

The child is probably the slowest cog in the daily activity machinery. He may even be the one who's holding up the parade; he's dragging his Reeboks. Unfortunately, threatening him, rushing him along, or discussing how time is fleeting is probably not going to move the situation forward substantially. A young child usually can't do too much (yet) about his inability to manage his time or even to understand where it goes. So the solution rests with Mom or Dad.

Parents can benefit mightily from some preplanning. Laying out the child's clothes and other school paraphernalia the night before is a big help. Your child should be involved and get used to helping. Even a three-year-old can do some things, such as picking out what toy she wants to take or deciding what color hat to wear. Here's one of the places where the other partner should come into the picture. One of you can make the lunch while the other lays out the clothes, or makes the discovery that there is no clean underwear. (Better to know today than tomorrow!). In fact, Dad may have better luck pulling things together if he's a new authoritative voice in the picture.

One of you can say, "Which overalls shall we lay out, the blue ones or the green ones?" By all means, limit the choices. Once you've laid out the wardrobe, you can get an idea of how much time will be needed for dressing and whether he can do some of it himself. Don't forget to lay out everything, including teddy bear, if that usually goes along to school. You can even use this time for a little extra naming of objects.

"Put your new brown shoes right here so that we'll be able to find them tomorrow."

"Here's *Listen to the Rain,* the book you wanted to take for Sharing Time. We'll get it all ready."

Anticipation today will pay big dividends in terms of smoother sailing tomorrow. So will choosing the kinds of clothes that are easy to get in and out of (see page 196). If it's snowsuit time, you'll have to allow for the time it takes to put on boots. Obviously the morning rush hour is no time to insist on a child dressing herself without any help. Still, you don't want to be doing it all. So why not pick one part for the child to do independently (such as putting on shoes) and allow plenty of time for it. More time can be spent on practice dressing on weekends.

Obviously, some things can't be anticipated, such as juice spilled on a clean shirt, sudden snow and the consequent search for boots, a last-minute phone call, or dozens of other things. But you can try. Because you're the one who understands time, you can set wake-up time to allow a few minutes extra so that everyone isn't breathless. Fifteen minutes less sleep isn't going to hurt anyone and it may make your schedule more manageable.

It will help if your own wardrobe decisions are made and you don't have to run out to the store at the last minute to get milk for breakfast. Every member of the family should do some preplanning.

One thing a good school can do is to establish a time schedule that suits the greatest number of parents. Meetings between parents and teachers at the beginning of the school year is one way to set this in place. A school should be able to be flexible enough to change its hours slightly if the majority of parents request it.

Teachers understand that scheduling, planning, and other time-related skills are valuable lessons to be learned at the preschool level and carried over into later school life. They establish a consistent daily rhythm so that children get used to the feel of blocks of time. A teacher will say, ''Time to clean up now,'' or ''Time we go to the park.'' Later, she may add, ''In one hour it will be time for lunch.'' She may point out, ''It usually takes us about ten minutes to clean up. Let's check the clock and see how long it takes us today.''

It doesn't matter what the clock says so much as that children get the idea that there is a time for things. Gradually they begin to see that snack time follows cleanup time, rest time follows lunchtime. They get a sense of order. And along with this comes a budding sense that certain routines take place not only at a certain time but within a certain time. Teachers know that younger children need help completing routines. So they help and encourage: ''You did a good job of putting your jacket on. Let me help you tie your shoes and we'll be all ready to go out.''

Parents and teachers working together can help children begin to understand routines and schedules. And they should try to reinforce what they teach by being good models on the issues of planning and completion of tasks.

A last word on timing. Some children seem to be born organized. Very early on, they will catch on to planning and thinking ahead. Some, on the other hand, march to the beat of their own drummer, which may not be beating in standard time. Dawdlers and dreamers need a gentle push in the direction of time awareness. Super-organized youngsters may need to learn how to relax and set their internal clocks for a little slower beat. A good preschool program will meet the needs of both kinds of children.

For their part, parents should not feel guilty about insisting that even three-year-olds join the family partnership and, to the extent of their capabilities, help get the show on the road.

DOWN TIME

So far we've been talking about "up time," the time of planning and doing. But everyone, grown-ups and children alike, needs time to relax. Too often we forget that "down time" is the important other side of the scheduling coin. Psychologists point out that people of all ages should have some time when they are doing something totally unstructured or nothing at all. It's a chance for a different set of three Rs—*reflection, refueling,* and *relaxation.*

But aren't children playing all day in preschool? Isn't that relaxation? Yes and no. Every day, and especially during the first weeks, a young child expends lots of energy adjusting to new people and coping with the new experiences of the preschool program. Think of it as if a grown-up were starting a new job and you get some idea of how taxing it can be.

One preschool teacher mentioned that one of the things young children don't get enough of in preschool is privacy. She pointed out that if they're in a center all day, they're forced to be with other children all the time. Then they come home and Mom and Dad want them to be with them to catch up on the events of the day. Often kids have no place during the day to just go off by themselves and ruminate. "We're going to build a privacy corner in our center," she says, "so children can go there for a few minutes and be by themselves if they want to."

If a child is in a half-day preschool program, a rest period or even a nap may be welcome. Many children go back to taking an afternoon nap for a while after they start half-day preschool. Gradually the nap dwindles to a rest and a time of quiet looking at books. It's only at about four and a half that children are able to get through a whole day of activity without falling apart in the early evening.

If a child is in a full-day program, she will almost always get a rest or nap at school. This doesn't mean that she doesn't need a little down time when she gets home. Kids are often tired when they come home from preschool. Organized afterschool activity—dancing, music lessons, religious instruction—may very well be too much for a young child. Certainly extensive shopping expeditions at the end of the day are probably better kept to a minimum, for your sake as well as for the child's. The same goes for afterschool parties. Visiting back and forth may be okay, particularly if you're sharing care cooperatively with another parent. But on these visits parents may find it works better to involve the kids in a quiet activity. This may be the time for TV watching, for looking at books, for sitting in the park for a few minutes if the weather is nice. It may be the time for a snack and sharing talk with parents and siblings or with the sitter or relative who's in charge of the child's care. Don't think of down time as a separate activity; it's simply nonorganized time that can be incorporated into the family's daily routine.

What is the preschool's responsibility for pacing and for down time? A good program catches the rhythm of the children in the class. "Each year's class is different," says Cele Mark, director of the Mekeel Early Childhood Center, in East Stroudsburg, Pennsylvania. Cele and her teachers watch for signs of fatigue that may signal that lunchtime or naptime should be moved up a bit. Some children have a great deal of energy, then burn out all of a sudden. If this is the way your child is, the teacher can help by pacing his activities. Again, share what you know. You may want to tell the teacher that at home Jessica seems to need a real sleep after lunch. Or a teacher may tell a parent, ''Robbie is very active all day in school. We have a hard time getting him to rest at naptime, and about the time you come to pick him up, he's a little overtired. We'll try to work on getting him to slow down. Meanwhile, you should probably give him an early supper and let him conk out.''

SLEEP

Preschool teachers say that sleep is a frequently discussed subject at parent meetings and teacher conferences. Parents want to know if their youngster is napping at school and for how long. They ask whether there is a right amount of sleep that every child should have or how they can get a youngster to sleep at night without a battle.

Sleep is a vital part of human life and growth. Every parent knows that a young child who hasn't had enough sleep falls apart. Most adults do the same thing. Outside of rare individuals like Thomas Edison, who was said to have required only three hours' sleep a night, most grown-ups need seven to eight hours and children need ten or more. In extreme situations, where humans are forced to be awake for long periods of time, their behavior changes radically. They become depressed, irrational, or physically ill. Sleep seems to be a way for us to recharge our internal batteries.

Children not only need more sleep than their parents, they have lower tolerance for missed sleep. It's important that they get what they need, both for their sakes and for the sanity of Mom and Dad. Sleep is also a vital factor in a child's getting the most out of preschool. On the most practical level, it's a waste of money to have your child in preschool only half awake.

That's why most full-time preschool programs include a naptime. Part-time programs (9:00–3:00) that include lunch often have a brief rest period after that meal.

A mother may ask, "How do you get Roger to nap after lunch? I can't seem to get him to do that at home." Preschool teachers have developed some good strategies for avoiding confrontation on the sleep issue. For one thing, in most settings they don't insist that children sleep. How, after all, can you *make* someone go to sleep? Teachers usually insist only that the children be engaged in quiet pastimes. Good preschool programs pack away noisy toys after lunch and bring out special "quiet boxes" and cuddle toys. They pull the shades or dim the lights and get out all the artifacts of sleep that each child needs—the blanket or doll, pacifier or, for younger children, a bottle. Some children will sleep, some won't. Those who don't sleep play without disturbing the nappers. Occasionally a rester will turn into a napper and vice versa.

This is also good practice at home. A child will often accept quiet time, but if you insist on bed, you'll get resistance. A four-year-old I know is a bundle of energy all morning and refuses to nap in a bed after lunch. But given a quiet time in her room, she'll often fall asleep on the floor and take a half-hour cat nap, much as a grown-up will fall asleep in front of the TV set or while reading in a chair.

But what about the youngster who can't last the morning in preschool and regularly puts his head down on the table in the late morning and falls asleep? A child who is sleepy by 11:00 A.M. may simply be a young person who needs more sleep than he is getting at night. Or it could be a sign of the wrong breakfast or no breakfast. Kids need to be fueled for the activity of preschool. But sweet breakfast foods (such as hot chocolate, sweet rolls, or cereal with marshmallows) give many children a short spurt of energy that then drops dramatically, usually around midmorning. That's one reason why preschools include a snack at 10:30 or so, as a sort of pit stop for those who need a little refueling. At home, a switch to another kind of breakfast— hot cereal, whole-grain bread with peanut butter, or scrambled eggs with a glass of plain (not chocolate) milk—can make a difference in your child's staying power during the morning (see "Food," in chapter 8).

However, a child who is constantly tired needs to be checked. If a teacher tells you that your child is dragging around or napping overtime and you know that he or she is getting ten hours of sleep or more at night and is eating well, then a visit to the doctor is in order.

When a child goes to preschool for a half day, a parent can usually pick up the new sleep rhythm by watching the child. It may be a matter of having lunch all ready when a youngster gets home and then popping him or her down for a nap or quiet time. It may be that the stimulation of preschool may eliminate naptime altogether and that supper is the meal that needs to be pushed up so that the preschooler can get to bed early.

PARENTS, SLEEP, AND ALL-DAY PRESCHOOL

All-day preschool sometimes presents a real dilemma for some parents in terms of sleep. You may not get home until 6:30 or 7:00 P.M. You haven't spent any time with your youngster. You have dinner together, and by that time it may be 8:30 or 9:00. Now your offspring has gotten a "second wind" and is revved up by your stimulating conversation or a roughhouse with one of you.

What's more important for a child, you ask, sharing

time or getting sleep? It probably depends on the child. Some children can manage on less sleep than others. If your youngster is one of those kids who bounces out of bed in the morning after a late dinner and shared family fun the night before, then you're lucky—and you're right. It is important for you and your son or daughter to have time together, and if you can only have it in the evening, then have it.

Some parents complain that a child who has been in preschool all day is overstimulated. One parent told us, ''My child comes home 'wired,' and it takes a long time for him to calm down and be ready for sleep. I notice, too, that he has trouble sleeping on Sunday nights before he goes to preschool.''

If your child comes home from a day at preschool constantly hyper and overstimulated, you may want to make a special effort to give him time to wind down. If this doesn't work, talk to his teacher or even spend a day at the preschool. Seeing him in action may help you figure out what's keeping him in overdrive. Maybe the program is putting a little too much pressure on him to do something he's not quite ready for. Or maybe he's just the kind of person who needs time to settle down. For this child—in fact, for almost any child—a quiet story before bedtime makes a lot of sense. Most children need a period of wind-down before they go to sleep.

Some parents are too rigid about sleep. Others have no rules, and their preschoolers, who are really not old enough to set their own bedtime rules, walk around like zombies at the child care center. Something in between is sensible. Set a bedtime and try to stay within a reasonable time frame. If a child is a poor sleeper, allow an extra half hour for her to settle down. Make sure that she has all her ritualistic sleep inducers—blanket, teddy, or whatever—even if it means you've had to cart this paraphernalia from home to preschool and back again. Story time before bedtime makes sense. A game of tag before bed does not.

FEEDBACK

Preschool may be the first place where you and your child haven't shared a block of time each day. You want to know what has been going on during those hours when you haven't been together. What is she doing? How is she doing? Is she happy? Is she eating? What is she learning? Very often she doesn't have anything tangible to show you and just as often she's close-mouthed about what she did in preschool. If you inquire, you may get something like this:

Mom: What did you do in school today, honey?

Alicia: Nothing.

Mom: Ah, come on, Alicia. You must have done something. Did you play with blocks? Did you go outside?

Alicia: No.

Mom: What did you have for lunch?

Alicia: We didn't have lunch.

Is it possible that your youngster had no food and no activity all day? Not likely. The reverse is probably true. She has had so many experiences that she can't single out one to tell you about. Or she hasn't incorporated her experiences into something she can talk about—yet. Two days or even two weeks from now you may get a fairly detailed rundown on today's activities. Or maybe you won't ever hear about this day's events. Either way, it doesn't mean that nothing happened or that it hasn't made an impression on Alicia. It just means that feedback from your child may be slow in coming.

Some children talk readily about what happened in

school. But often, especially with young children who don't have much vocabulary, their stories don't make a lot of sense. Take the young person who told her father she had put her hamburger on the shelf and was saving it for tomorrow! It took a while for Dad to figure out that she meant plastic play food and not the real thing.

Parents and children need to reflect together on some of the things that happen during the time you are apart, but how do you get feedback from your child? One way you may be able to get a little more information from your youngster is to ask your questions while you're still in the center or other preschool setting. If there's a jack-o'-lantern, and you say, "Oh, look at the pumpkin head," you may get to hear the story of how they scooped out the seeds. If you say, "What a great block house," you may get to hear the saga of the construction. Being right in the room where it all happened may remind a child of something he or she wants to share. Then all you have to do is to be an interested listener. A technique one parent finds works is to throw out a few wild ideas about what may have happened:

"I'll bet you rode a dinosaur in school today, didn't you?"

The child answers, "No, we didn't. But we . . ."

Another parent found that the way in can be through inquiring about how his friend's day went. However you make the inquiry, it's important not to push too much.

Some children just don't talk as much as others. They may be getting as much out of preschool as their more voluble peers, but they don't tell you about it. In this case a good teacher, knowing that your youngster is one of the reticent ones and knowing how much parents value feedback, may give you a capsule picture of your son's or daughter's day at pickup time. A teacher may say, "Aaron had a wonderful time with Play-Doh today." Or, "Barbara went down the slide for the first time today."

If the teacher doesn't volunteer this kind of information, you can ask. Sometimes a specific question gives the teacher a frame. "Does Raoul still love to feed the rabbit?" focuses the teacher on what Raoul did, and you'll get a more specific answer than if you asked, "Did Raoul have a good time today?" Make sure you choose your moment to ask thoughtfully. If she's dealing with a problem of an upset child elsewhere in the room, for example, this would be a day to skip your request.

A little daily communication between parent and teacher is a good way to keep in touch with how your child is doing. Even if it's only a few words, it can make a big difference in your child's comfort at home and at school. For example, a teacher may call a parent aside:

Teacher: I thought I would let you know that Justin had a hard day today. He and Danny had quite a fight, and we had to separate them. Danny's out-of-control behavior frightened Justin, and he may want to talk to you about it.

Parent: Should I ask him?

Teacher: Why don't you let him bring it up. I just wanted you to be aware of the incident.

Justin (later at home): I hate that school. And I hate Danny.

Parent: Yes, you had some trouble today. Want to tell me about it?

Communication about a specific event or incident sometimes comes from the child, sometimes from a parent, sometimes from a teacher. You should feel comfortable enough at a good preschool to have some form of daily communication between yourself and the teachers of your preschooler. Where this isn't possible, a newsletter, a weekly note, or some other form of touching base is important.

Sometimes preschools either send home a brief daily note on your child's day or post it on the bulletin board. Sometimes these notes merely tell you what your child had for lunch and whether she took a nap. But often they are more anecdotal and will say, "We collected leaves today," or "We walked to the river and saw two tugboats and an ocean liner." The value of these short notes is that you are kept up-to-date on what is going on in the preschool and you have a talking point with your child. If there is no daily note board in your child's preschool, you may want to suggest that the teachers start one.

SCHOOL CONFERENCES

What about more formal communication? Shouldn't there be a special time and place for parents and teachers to talk and/or exchange ideas?

The school conference is the place for this kind of sharing. It's here that you will find out how the school thinks your child is doing. A conference is a place to bring up what is going on at home that may affect your child's behavior. It is a place to air gripes or to discuss concerns. Given the fact that children often behave differently at home and at school, it is important to have a time for putting the home/school picture together.

Some preschools have a regularly scheduled conference several times during the school year. Other programs supplement annual or semiannual conferences with parent get-togethers and/or monthly newsletters. A preschool that doesn't have some provision for conferences is usually not worth considering.

The ideal parent-teacher conference is one where the

teacher talks individually with the person who is the child's primary caregiver. In some families this is Mom, in others it's Dad. But it could be Grandma or Aunt Sally or a housekeeper or caregiver. These days good preschools often encourage caregivers as well as parents to be present at a conference. This makes a lot of sense. If the housekeeper is a significant other person in a child's life, she should be there. If both parents are sharing care of a child, it's good to have both parents present at the conference.

Most conferences between parents and teachers are routine. Almost everything is a fair subject for a conference —food preferences, temper tantrums, daily schedules, learning patterns, separation, toilet training, and a battery of other subjects of concern to parents and teachers. The conference is the proper place to find out how your child is doing, what she's doing, and what you can do to help things along. It's also the place where parents may get a surprising view of their child from a completely different angle. It could go like this:

Teacher: We enjoy Sherry so much. She's so lively.

Mom: Sherry *lively*? But she's so withdrawn at home.

Teacher: Maybe not so withdrawn as quiet. I know you live far away from neighbors. I think Sherry is really responding to having other children around.

During this particular conference, the parent and the teacher talked about the blossoming of Sherry. The parent wanted to know if she should provide playmates for Sherry at home as well as at school. The school thought that Sherry was probably getting as much stimulation as she needed for now. But after the conference Sherry's mother knew much more about her little girl than she had previously, and perhaps she looked at her somewhat differently. Parents can definitely benefit from seeing their young person through someone else's eyes.

Here's another possible conference scenario:

Mom/Dad: Kevin says he likes school, but every Monday he says he feels sick.

Director: Janet [the teacher] thinks Kevin is a little overwhelmed. Don't forget, he's practically the youngest four-year-old in his group and he tends to have a shorter attention span. He's easily distracted, so we try to minimize the hullabaloo for him. Janet is working with him alone for a few minutes a day. We're hoping that when he gets more confident about doing puzzles and other small motor activities, he'll be more independent and be able to stick to an activity for a longer period of time.

Mom/Dad: What can we do to help?

Teacher: You might want to spend some time reading to him or playing games. Encourage him to finish what he starts, but keep the activities short.

HOW TO CONFERENCE SUCCESSFULLY

Most preschools see parents at least twice a year for a conference. The date is usually set by the teacher for a time that's convenient for everyone. A lot of what goes on at a conference depends on the style of both teacher and school. Good teachers understand that often when a parent goes to see a child, the parent may suddenly feel like a child being called down to the principal's office. Teachers may have some of those "called on the carpet" feelings themselves.

One teacher said, "As my role as teacher becomes more defined, the parents value my judgment more. Teachers need to build parents' confidence and vice versa. But still, everyone feels a little bit on the spot when conference time rolls around. Teachers feel stress, especially if there is a problem that needs airing. It's easy for both parent and school to get into a pattern of blaming the other for the situation. But it's much more constructive for the child they're both trying to help if everyone can focus on a solution to the problem." In other words, frankness is paramount. Blame is unnecessary. The important thing is for everyone to get beyond personal feelings and move the situation forward, for the child's sake.

Here are a few things you can do to get the most out of a conference:

▲ Set a time that's convenient for both you and the teacher, and for your spouse if at all possible. Don't try to sandwich a school conference between errands or into a lunch hour, or you'll feel harassed. If you have another child, try to get a sitter (sometimes a preschool will have sitters available during conference times).

• Have some idea of what you're going to ask about. Prepare a list of questions if necessary. Here are some samples that may help:

"How is Debby doing with her bladder control? I know she had an accident or two the first weeks of school."

"Sam mentioned that he hates to paint and he never brings home painting. How are you handling that?"

"I have a hard time with Nellie about food at home. Any suggestions on how I can get her to eat?"

"Eddie seems to need a lot of physical exercise. Is he getting enough in school?"

▪ Start by talking about some of the things you like about the program and/or the teacher. This will not only get the conference off on an upbeat note, it will give the teacher a little better view of you.

▲ Listen carefully to what the teacher is saying. Keep

in mind that she's a professional and has seen many children in action.

• Be aware that you and she are sharing ideas. One of you shouldn't be doing all the talking. You should especially try to share whatever is going on at home that you think might affect your child in school.

▪ Try to keep to the time allotted for the conference. There may be other parents waiting to hear about their children.

▲ Establish a time for another meeting or at least a phone call if an issue needs follow-up. If your youngster is having separation problems, for example, you might say, "I'll call you next week to check on how it's going."

Occasionally an issue comes up that won't wait for a regular conference time. Then a note or a phone call between parent and teacher or director is in order. It can be initiated in either direction and it can either settle the matter or call for a meeting. Common sense needs to come into play here; you can't take up the teacher's time endlessly. But most of the teachers we talked to did not complain about too many parent communiqués; rather they complained about too few. "We need to know what's going on at home, what parents are thinking," says Mary Hayes, director of the Children's Underground. And Ann-Marie Mott, director of the Bank Street Lower School, says that talking with parents helps the school to do its job.

We have spoken before about the teacher's perspective, that fresh eye that can reveal something the parents were too close to see. Here's a story that illustrates it:

The teacher was concerned. Matt had a fabulous vocabulary and a wide frame of reference. And yet he seemed to have trouble doing some very simple things, such as turning a doorknob. At the conference the director spoke to Matt's parents about his physical ineptitude. They said they'd noticed it, but didn't think it was important. After all, he was so bright. The director suggested that the preschool wanted to see Matt develop in every way, not just intellectually. She explained that it was important for him to know how to use his hands—for sports, for games, for writing later on.

Matt's parents admitted they hadn't thought of it just that way. They'd been so involved in Matt's intellectual accomplishments. They asked what they could do.

Parents and teacher worked on getting Matt to use his body as well as his mind. And he developed better coordination, but it took a full year before he did the routine physical things that his peers were able to do easily. It almost seems as if children can't grow in all directions at once. Matt's folks, being educators themselves, were very interested in his mental achievement. Fortunately, good preschool programs look at every facet of a child's growth and development.

BRINGING PRESCHOOL HOME

Karen comes home from school with Daddy. When she gets in the door, she says, "I'll put my coat in the closet. A closet is something like a cubby."

Children catch on quickly to likenesses between school and home. They readily bring home food menus, housekeeping details, and other day-to-day routines. But kids aren't the only ones who can use the school as a model for certain things at home. As we've said before, one of the great fringe benefits of preschool is that if you hang around there even a little bit, you'll pick up some good pointers on how to share some of the best parts of school at home. Even if you don't, your boy or girl may show you the way. ''Why didn't I think of that?'' you may say as your child shows you how a visit to the store can be turned into a fabulous learning experience. There's a good reason why you didn't do it and the teacher did. The teacher is a professional; it's her business. But you're missing out on one of the great ''perks'' of preschool if you don't pick up on some of the ideas your child carries home with him.

A simple yet crucial example of this is what you can observe about the ways teachers and children talk with and question each other. Simply talking with your child is a much undervalued learning experience. Take your cue from how a good teacher conducts Circle Time (or whatever it's called in your preschool program). This is the time when children and teacher sit together and share ideas about a story or the snow falling or anything else that's going on. One grandmother caregiver says, ''I see how they do it in the school. Now I make it a point to share with my grandchild while she's watching TV. That way she gets more out of it. Sometimes we just talk about the program. Other times I'll ask her what's happening on the screen. Sometimes we talk about the commercials. It helps her to understand the images, and I get a better understanding of how she sees things.''

One of the things you may observe in a good preschool program is the way, under the guidance of a good teacher, everyday experiences turn into opportunities for learning. With a little practice, you can do the same thing at home.

For example, while you're setting the table for dinner, you might ask your preschooler, ''Let's use the red mats tonight. Can you get me *three* red mats from the drawer?'' Or at another time you might say, ''I need to sort the laundry. Let's take out all the socks and put together the ones that are the same.'' This kind of relaxed togetherness with a little sorting and classifying thrown in not only fits into busy schedules, it gives a youngster a sense of accomplishment and reinforces concepts he is learning in school.

But as the song says, "It ain't what you do, it's the way that you do it." That's particularly true when it comes to parent-and-child talk. Recently I was introduced to a charming, bright four-year-old whose parent immediately began, "Josh, this is our friend Barbara Brenner. What letter does her first name begin with? What letter does her last name begin with? Do you hear the *B* sound?" And so on, until that young citizen must have wished fervently that the lady with the *B* names had never come on the scene.

The letter *B* in my name is less interesting (I hope) than some of the things this child and I could have been talking about. In other words, children don't need drill-talk. They need meaningful, down-to-earth conversation—with them, not at them. How you use language, how you help your child on a problem-solving task, how you expand on what your child says, how you ask the kinds of questions that encourage a youngster to think and speak—that's what a parent can do to enrich the preschool time at home.

WHAT KIND OF TOYS AT HOME?

Parents often ask whether they should duplicate some of the toys that are in preschool at home. You certainly don't want to replicate the preschool. For one thing, there's a certain freshness and novelty about a toy or piece of equipment that's only available at school. There's another good reason not to try to bring most nursery equipment home. It tends to be hideously expensive. However, certain staples of the nursery school setting bear repeating at the house. One example is a trunk of dress-up clothes. That has play value at home as well as at school, and the differences in the items will make it a totally different experience.

A set of good sturdy blocks and Legos belong at home as well as at school. Blocks are so abstract themselves that their play value is endless. Many kids play with their blocks at school in one way and at home in another. School block play often emphasizes group constructions; at home a child builds things on his own. Both experiences are valuable, and they "build" on each other, in every sense. Puzzles and age-appropriate games also enhance home play-learning. They don't have to be the same ones that the child plays with at school. For guidance on toys for preschoolers, you might want to read *Buy Me! Buy Me!* by Joanne Oppenheim.

BOOKS AT HOME

As for books, they should be a fixture at home—as familiar as the kitchen faucet or the TV. We know one family that even takes books traveling. They go along in the car to the dentist, to the laundromat, on trips—always available to enjoy and share with the children at any time. Better than candy for fussy times—and much more nourishing!

Another way to help reinforce the book connection a youngster makes at preschool is to pay regular visits to the local library. The book-borrowing habit can't be acquired too early. Children love to borrow from the library the books they know from preschool. There's a kind of magic for a child in seeing a favorite like *Make Way for Ducklings* or *A Chair for My Mother* in the library as well as at preschool and to know that she can take it home and keep it for a while. Or she may discover a new favorite that will be checked out until both of you can recite it by heart. Perhaps it will even go to school for show-and-tell. When parents, preschool, and child share book ideas, it can't help but implant a love of reading.

In addition to going to the public library, every child

Sharing books is a preschool experience that parents and children can bring home.

should have his own collection of books that can be added to from year to year. A few of the many books that children of three and four will enjoy reading over and over again are *The Little Red Hen* (in any of its many versions); *Curious George,* by H. A. Rey; *Pierre,* by Maurice Sendak; *The Tale of Peter Rabbit,* by Beatrix Potter; and a collection of poetry such as *Poems to Read to the Very Young,* selected by Josette Frank. But keep in mind that in the case of books for children three to five, as in the case of toys, less is more. A youngster of three to five will get more out of the book connection if there isn't a glut and if they aren't pushed too eagerly.

Reading with your child is surely one of the places home and school can reinforce each other and enrich both you and your child. Early familiarity and enjoyable experiences with magazines, books, and newspapers have been proven to be accurate predicters of a good lifelong relationship with books. That's certainly a good reason for

162

reading with your preschooler, even though she gets books aplenty in school. The main reason you should read to your child is simply that it's great fun. Preschool or teacher can never take the place of the few minutes every evening with a loving parent. Sharing a book while on a parent's lap is a different experience from sharing a book with the kids or the teacher at preschool. Even the same book will have different resonance when a child hears the story at home. It's not a lesson in reading readiness that you're after. View it as a literary experience!

One other point: Don't underestimate the importance of "modeling" the reading habit. Read yourself and watch how even an eighteen-month-old will copycat the process.

To sum up, it is ideal if some of the things that happen at school also happen at home, to form part of a seamless whole. This does not mean that teachers should try to be parents or that parents should try to be teachers. It simply means that neither learning nor play needs to stop when a child leaves preschool and comes home. Relaxed, pleasant time together, parent and child, is the other piece of pre-school.

PRESCHOOL POLICY IN ACTION

Discipline

Discipline is very much a part of every preschool program. But how teachers maintain order and handle misbehavior is the difference between a good program and one with serious shortcomings.

As we've already said, discipline should be one of the things you talk about very early in your interviews with a school. But sometimes parents are a little hesitant about asking directly, especially if they're unsure themselves about what to look for. Because discipline is tricky, everyone has a personal view of both its meaning and its application. For example, one parent told us, ''I was horrified when I discovered that they had a 'bad' corner in my child's nursery school, and that he was being placed there for disciplining!'' Standing a youngster in the ''bad'' corner is something this parent disapproves of strongly. But another parent said proudly that his daughter had never had to sit in the ''bad'' corner, but that he approved of the idea as a disciplinary measure. Who's wrong and who's right?

In fact, good preschools have better ways of handling a young child than ''cornering'' him and calling him ''bad.'' In most cases where everything else is in place—caring teachers, a developmentally appropriate program, plenty of space to run around in, and all the other elements of a good program that we keep talking about—discipline will be in keeping with the quality of the rest of the program. Here's what you should expect:

The teachers will maintain a decent amount of order as they help the children toward self-discipline. They'll protect your child from another child who doesn't yet have sufficient self-control and protect that child from himself so that all the children feel safe. They'll step in to mediate a dispute when it's necessary and let the children handle it when it's not. They'll see to it that certain rules are laid down and kept. And where misbehavior requires action, they'll take positive steps without damaging any youngster's self-esteem.

What are some specific discipline techniques that you may see in action in your youngster's preschool and may want to emulate at home? Often you'll see a teacher distract a child who is doing something unacceptable. Distraction is a good basic tool of early childhood and can avoid many a head-on confrontation. Instead of "No, Billy, you can't have that," you'll see a teacher hand Billy another book and say something like, "Sandy is looking at that book, Billy. Here's one for you."

Preschoolers, especially younger ones, are not ready for long lectures or explanations about behavior. They need short, clear directives, and not too many. That's why, in a good preschool setting, you won't find a teacher or aide giving a lengthy explanation about the fact that everyone should hold hands when they go outside so that no one will get lost or be left behind or get run over by a car. The teacher is more likely to say, "Everyone grab your part-ner's hand. Make a chain. Here we go." Simple. To the point. And with the expectation that it will be done.

Good discipline—home or school—doesn't usually mean punishing misbehavior so much as it means avoiding it or setting sensible rules for important things and making sure that they are followed. However, there are times when misbehavior does have to be dealt with.

One of the most effective forms of discipline for young children that both parents and teachers can usually agree on is a brief period of isolation. Whether you call it "grounding," as does one preschool, or "thinking time," as does another, the point is the same. A child who is trou-blesome or disruptive is asked to leave the group and to have a period of time out for reflection or calming down. A teacher or aide may even accompany the child so that it seems not a punishment but a true "time away."

"I find it pretty effective," says one teacher. "It can break a cycle of misbehavior. And I always try to give the child the decision as to when to return to the group. 'When you're ready to settle down. When you've had a chance to think about this. When you're ready to play without hurting anyone.' That puts the ball in the child's court and helps her save face.''

BRINGING SCHOOL DISCIPLINE HOME

There's another issue that's important here—the match between home and school discipline. Families differ in their child-rearing practices. Some families are softies—they're permissive with their children. Others are toughies and run authoritarian households. And some are in between these two extremes. They're the authoritative parents who have clear rules but allow their kids some decision making and who reason more than punish. Healthy youngsters can come out of any of these three approaches. But according to most research, it is the middle-of-the-road style that usually gets the best results.

Whatever your personal style, the discipline philosophy you feel comfortable with in raising your child should be somewhat consistent with that of the preschool. If there's a wide gap between what you believe and what the school believes, your youngster can only get confused, and the most important rules of discipline in both settings may go unlearned.

One teacher said that her biggest disciplinary problems stem from parents who laugh at a child's misbehavior. Another teacher said, ''Sometimes a parent will tell us to hit a child. They'll say, 'If she doesn't behave, give her a smack.' This puts me in a difficult position. I personally don't believe in hitting children.''

In the old days youngsters got smacked around a lot. Nowadays enlightened communities have outlawed hitting or spanking and other forms of physical punishment. In New York State, for example, it is against the law for a preschool teacher to strike a child. It's considered child abuse and is grounds for the teacher's dismissal.

167

There are, however, a surprising number of states that still permit teachers to hit children. These laws could apply even in preschools, although no good early childhood setting will take advantage of this nasty legal loophole. This is one of the issues where there's a clear right and wrong. It's wrong, and dangerous, for anyone to hit young children. Parents should neither do it themselves nor condone or suggest it. Never ask a teacher to discipline your child by physical punishment. Just as much to be avoided are cruel or punishing phrases—"You're so stupid," "I can't stand you"—words that sting and break down a youngster's sense of self-worth. We have a sign at Bank Street that speaks to this. It says, "Sticks and stones will break my bones, but words can break my heart." Professional teachers know how to maintain discipline without having to resort to physical punishment or mental abusiveness.

In general, spanking, hitting, and other forms of physical punishment are forms of discipline both parents and caregivers should avoid. It is very easy to get exasperated with a young child at times. We've all done it. And if you blow your cool occasionally, it is not going to mark your offspring for life. However, if you find that the impulse to hit is coming often or your child is out of control more often than she's in, then you'll want to ask yourself, "Is my discipline method working?"

This is one place where the teacher-parent partnership can be particularly helpful. You may want to find out how the preschool fosters good behavior. Talking with the teacher about discipline can be especially helpful if you see that your child behaves better at school than she does at home. Sometimes the teacher will offer you material on discipline. Or she may invite you to sit in for a morning and watch how the school handles discipline. Never be afraid to ask for a better way.

WHAT PARENTS CAN DO

Always try to clear up the discipline question before your child starts school. But if the issue comes up at any time, it needs talking about. Based on something your child reports, you can ask the teacher a direct question: "How do you discipline children when they misbehave?" or "Do you discipline a child who wets his pants?" or "We don't believe in making an issue out of eating. How do you feel about it?" or "How do you handle it when a child hits another child?"

Keep an open mind during these exchanges. Often teachers have a good idea of what kind of discipline works with your child. But sometimes what a preschool says is not borne out in practice. If your youngster tells you something disturbing about discipline in her preschool, you need to respond immediately. If she is being hit, shamed, or punished severely, you'd better get in there right away and take a look at what is going on. Here's an example based on a true incident:

Brian came home very upset one day. He told his father that the teacher had hit him. The father, understandably disturbed, went directly to the teacher in question and to the director of the school. The director questioned the teacher, who unequivocally denied hitting the child. The director was extremely concerned over the incident but was convinced of the teacher's reliability. Meanwhile, by the next day Brian seemed to have forgotten all about it. Not only did he not respond to further questions, his relations with the teacher resumed their former good status.

The teacher and director spent the next week trying to

figure out where Brian's story had come from. Had Brian fantasized it? Had the teacher read the group a story in which someone got hit? Was Brian angry with the teacher because she had asked him to stop some activity or to do something he didn't want to do? Had Brian done something as yet undetected that made him think he deserved to be hit?

To this day, no one has been able to figure out what went through three-year-old Brian's head that day. But the point is, both parent and preschool took action, because they care about Brian.

Many tales children tell about hitting or other violence are *not* true. It isn't that they lie deliberately; it's simply that they cannot altogether see the difference between fantasy and real life, so parents have to be careful in accepting what their youngsters say.

If a child reports something disturbing from school, however, it needs to be investigated right away, even if you suspect your son or daughter is "crying wolf." It's not easy to assess whether a young child is telling an accurate story, but you can't afford not to check it out. Start by going through the regular school channels that we've suggested in the section on conferencing. Chances are you'll get to the bottom of it that way. But if you don't, you'll need to pursue the matter in other ways (see "When You and the Preschool Disagree," in chapter 9). For a health or safety matter, or something that may involve a criminal charge, such as child abuse, you will need to call your local community agency that handles the rights of children to find out how to proceed.

No Fighting, No Biting

What does a good preschool do about play fighting, real fighting, and other issues where children are hurting (or at least could potentially hurt) one another? What should a parent do to support the school?

Few preschools these days encourage kids to fight it out, but some don't come down as hard on the side of law and order as others do. The same is true of parents. Some parents get violent on the subject of toy guns in a preschool. Some teachers feel the same way. But the teachers and parents are not always in the same place at the same time. And regardless of how you feel about gun play at the kiddie corral, chances are that the way the school handles it will be the model your youngster will follow.

At Bank Street's preschool the teachers encourage the peaceful solution of conflicts and discourage shoot-'em-up games. Children don't tote gun hardware or any of the other war toys so aggressively promoted on television while they are in school. If they have them, they learn to leave them at home. But don't kids have to get that aggression out of their systems? Sure, and there's plenty of chance for rough-and-tumble in the rooftop play yard. Plenty of cowboys and cowgirls running and jumping. But it's done without guns.

This is consistent with other parts of our program, which focuses on, among other things, developing social skills for use in the real world. The school reasons that preschool is not too soon for youngsters to get the idea that slugging it out or shooting it out is not the best way of solving problems. Teachers occasionally gently remind two- and three-year-olds that "there's no pushing in school" or "no fighting."

A case in point. On a recent morning two youngsters were improvising guns from plastic Lego toys. This was the conversation:

Child (to teacher): I wish I had a real gun.

Teacher: We don't have any guns here.

And then when the kids kept on banging away, the teacher said, simply, "No gun play."

Obviously the issue here is broader than whether you allow your child to play with guns or whether you want him to hit back when he's hit. One reason why most good preschools discourage children from fighting or from playing violent games that are likely to hurt someone is not a matter of philosophy; it's one of safety. Where there's a puncher or zapper, there's a punchee or zappee. Young children, unfortunately, don't understand that there are defensive and offensive hits or that it's okay to play-shoot your friend but you don't play-shoot your grandma who has a heart condition. Young children can't even really grasp the notion that a play gun and a real gun are not the same. So there's a real possibility that children can hurt themselves or someone else.

Danger aside, there's a housekeeping problem for teachers when there are no holds barred. You can't really get the most from a preschool program when youngsters are at each other. Life tends to focus around the combatants, and although you could say that children learn something from every experience, there's a limit to this kind of learning.

Keep in mind that one of the aims of preschool is to help children find better ways of resolving conflicts than by bopping each other. Helping them to develop language is one way. If a youngster can't yet talk about what's happening, the teacher will step in.

For example, two kids may be fighting over a toy. The teacher may say, "Sandy, what's happening here?"

That gets Sandy to stop tugging or shoving and explain, "Alex took my telephone, and I had it first."

The teacher may ask, "Can you share it?" And if Sandy doesn't think so, she may say, "Well, then, you'd better tell Alex how you feel about it."

Replacing action with thought and appropriate language is an important learning accomplishment. That's why you'll often notice preschool teachers intervening between two combatants with the admonition to "use your words."

To sum up, the young person who plays with guns is not doomed to be a gangster. Nor is the child who grows up in a center that puts the lid on combat going to be a wimp. However, there is a lot of mileage for both children in learning to work out conflicts in other ways. Sooner or later, all kids need to learn that you can't punch, bite, or shoot your way to the top, but that you can't run away from a challenge either. The sooner a youngster learns control, and strategies for solving disagreements, the freer he is to concentrate on other skills. Certainly you as a parent have to do your part in supporting harmony in the center. If your youngster's preschool has a rule against guns, make sure that your boy or girl leaves that hardware at home.

WHAT THE TEACHER DOES

An incident we witnessed at a preschool underscores how important the issue of aggressive behavior can be. Two children were playing quietly. All of a sudden one youngster swooped in and bit the other youngster on the leg. The child who was bitten was understandably very upset. The teacher who witnessed the biting couldn't have done anything to prevent the incident; it happened too fast. One teacher took the crying child to the bathroom to wash the wound. The head teacher concentrated on the biter, telling him in a straightforward way that he could not hurt other people. Further, she did something else: she made him responsible for his actions. While she acted as mediator between aggressor and victim, not only was the child made to look at the bite mark on the other child's leg, he was asked to get ice for it and to help make her more comfortable.

No one attempted to make a pariah of this four-year-old. At the same time, he got the clear message that his behavior was totally unacceptable and that he had to make amends by helping his victim. One teacher said about the incident: "You need to make sure that the response is timely, productive, and appropriate."

When we left, the two youngsters were playing together amicably. Will the biter strike again? It's hard to say. The teacher will keep a close watch on both children—on the biter to observe whether he tries to bite often, which may signify problems; and on the child who was bitten, to see that she recovers from the experience.

Some children are naturally more rambunctious, more physical, than others. Some of this excess energy may come out in shoot-'em-up play, hit-and-run games, or downright ghoulish pastimes. A certain amount of this comes under the heading of "kids will be kids." At the same time, like other uncivilized behavior, it may need to be toned down. And when it violates another children's rights, it has to be stopped in no uncertain terms.

On the other end of the spectrum are youngsters who can't or won't defend themselves or who continually seem to be victims. A good teacher watching this behavior will try to help this kind of child be more assertive and try to figure out why he can't defend himself. At the same time she'll protect him when she thinks he needs it.

If children get a clear idea of their own and other people's rights at home, they're much less apt either to be victims or to victimize others at school. Parents should encourage kids' getting along without fighting. They should discourage fisticuffs. But occasionally it happens that, for whatever reason, the message you've tried to deliver has not gotten through (yet) to a youngster. One day you may get a call from the preschool that your young person is always fighting. He is considered by the other children and their parents to be a bully. Or your youngster doesn't seem to be able to stand up for his rights at all, and he's always being put upon.

It may be upsetting, humiliating, and even infuriating for a parent to be on the receiving end of this type of phone call. At the same time, you should know that this is one of the most typical preschool scenarios, and it's a great service to you that the preschool wants to help you help your child. You may have already suspected that Roger is a little too quick with his hands or that Jennifer just won't ever stand up for her rights. This is one of the places where a good teacher can give you insights about your child and new ways of discipline that you can use to change his or her behavior.

HEALTH

The parent was shocked. Her child was in a good preschool. She had checked it out and everything seemed in place. Her own child had met all the entry health requirements —medical exam, up-to-date immunization—and she assumed that everyone else had met the health requirements too. First her youngster came home with pinworms. Then it was head lice.

Is there any way you can prevent this from happening in preschool? Probably not, as long as your child is hanging out with other children. Germs, viruses, and—yes— even head lice tend to get passed around. The bad news is that your youngster is liable to get more childhood diseases and exotic infections as a result of going to preschool than if she stayed home. The good news is that she'll probably get over the typical childhood diseases at an early age rather than in grade school. And the other trade-off is that she'll have a lot of interesting and stimulating times. You'll have to decide what you think the cost-benefit ratio is.

Some preschools send children home if morning inspection shows them to be sniffly. But many child care centers don't make any special effort to keep children with colds isolated. They say that if a child isn't really sick with a cold, it's difficult and fruitless to try to prevent contact with other children.

Good preschool centers look the children over every morning and if someone looks ill, he or she is checked out further. Licensed child centers must do this by law. Still, it's no guarantee that chicken pox, pinworms, or lice won't invade a preschool. The real question is whether children who are ill or who have something contagious should be brought to school. A well-run child care center, nursery school, or preschool has clear rules about when a child should be kept home. At our Bank Street setting there is a nurse on staff who helps parents make decisions about health matters. But some decisions are harder to make than others. Some parents who work have a hard time arranging for an alternate sitter if a youngster is sick. What happens is that sometimes a child who complains at home of a headache or stomachache is brought to school with the promise that "it will go away." And indeed, sometimes it does. But sometimes the headache is a first sign of flu or some other contagious disease and the child needs to be home.

▲ ■ ●

WHAT PARENTS CAN DO

Here are some steps you can follow to maximize good health in your child's preschool:

Exchange important information with your center director when you register your child for day care.

1. Provide important phone numbers.

- ▲ Where you can be reached during the day.
- • Your family physician and hospital of choice.
- ▪ Person to contact in an emergency in case you can't be reached. (This could be the person you have selected as alternative caregiver—a relative, neighbor, friend, or other dependable adult.)

2. Provide the director with any special information he or she should have about your child's medical history. For example:

- ▲ Has your child had any serious illnesses?
- • Is your child taking any medication?
- ▪ Does your child have allergies that you know of?

3. Provide the center director with a copy of your child's immunization record and the results of the latest annual medical checkup. (You can obtain this from your physician.) The director will keep this record in your child's permanent folder.

4. If your child has had measles or mumps, give your center director a note from your physician indicating the date of this illness.

When a disease occurs, take steps to minimize risk and to control the illness:

1. Tell the school if your child is exposed to a contagious disease.

2. Keep your child at home if he or she develops symptoms that may endanger the health of other children.
Note : We know it isn't practical or realistic to expect parents to keep children home every time they have a runny nose. But with some symptoms, a child may endanger his own health and the health of the other children and staff by being in preschool when he is sick. Your preschool should be able to tell you what these are.

3. Take appropriate action if your child is diagnosed as having any contagious disease.

4. Be sure to follow your preschool's policies related to special disease-control needs.

Try to keep your youngster in good health by making sure that he or she has plenty of rest and a good diet. If a school has a firm health policy (such as keeping a child home if she has a contagious disease), follow the rules, even if it's tough on you. It simply isn't fair to infect other children.

If your child will be going to preschool all day, and if both parents are working, make plans for sick-day care before school starts. Whether it's Grandma, a sitter, a neighbor, a friend, or a child care center set up specifically for youngsters who are temporarily ill, you should have an alternative plan worked out so that you don't feel pressure to send your youngster to school when there's any question about his health.

Teach your child basic health habits as early as possible. According to health professionals, hand washing is *the* most important health habit to instill in a child. It's even more important than tooth brushing. Help the teacher by enforcing hand washing at home, especially before meals and after toileting. Make sure that your youngster gets adequate sleep and a good breakfast before going off to school. Diet is clearly a factor in resistance to disease, as is rest.

THE PRESCHOOL'S RESPONSIBILITY

Otherwise healthy children are at risk in any school setting from a number of communicable diseases. According to Dr. Steven Mehran, senior medical consultant to the New York City Department of Health, having infection-control procedures in place in school is imperative. According to this physician, every preschool should have readily available:

- ▲ Running water (for hand washing by children and teachers)
- • Soap (for same)
- ▪ Paper towels (for drying, then throwing away)
- ▲ Household bleach (for mixing with water to disinfect toys and surfaces)
- • First-aid kit (for treating cuts, and so on)

As we've already said, hand washing is the key. Health care professionals advise that both adults and children should wash hands:

- ▲ When they arrive at school
- • Any time child or teacher is involved with toileting
- ▪ Before eating any food
- ▲ After any contact with body fluids (this means any time teacher wipes a child's nose, cleans off a cut or scrape, wipes tears, and so on)

What about teachers using gloves? Some doctors recommend the use of gloves if a teacher is giving first aid—in other words, where blood is involved. Other doctors are concerned that putting on the gloves will get to be more important than responding to what may be an emergency situation. One teacher asked, "If I use gloves when I touch a child, won't the child get the wrong idea about her own bodily fluids?"

Dr. Mehran thinks it's useful to teach young children that it is dangerous to handle blood—*anyone's* blood. He's in favor of integrating safe health habits into the preschool curriculum, though he does not advocate a special health curriculum for the AIDS crisis (see page 251).

SAFETY

Parents ask, "How can I make sure our preschool is taking every precaution and that I won't have to worry about the safety of my child?"

Directors respond, "We are very careful about equipment, sharp corners, security. But still, accidents do happen. How can I reassure parents and still be realistic?"

A good preschool keeps an eye out for potential hazards. Inside, heavy furniture is firmly anchored; corners of tables are rounded; there are few breakables and no swallowables within reach. If there's an outdoor play area at the school, it's often divided into age areas, so that stumbling two-year-olds won't run into trikes powered by older children or be clouted by a swing. Health and safety regulations are part of the licensing requirements for certain kinds of preschool settings in many states, but even where they're not, any teacher who has her degree in early childhood education has been schooled in health and safety.

Supervision is the other piece of the health and safety picture. Good teachers have a sixth sense about where chil-

dren are in a room and if they're in a potentially dangerous situation. That's a matter of experience and training
—which is why having trained people with your youngster
is so important.

But in spite of good teachers and safe equipment, accidents do happen. Kids fall, they bump themselves and each
other, they get a cut or a bruise as they play. One reason
for this high accident rate in preschool is that most children from two through five are not fully coordinated. They
blunder and stumble around as they work on both independence and control. Does this mean that a good preschool is
one that reins in this experimentation? Not at all. Trying
is an invaluable part of learning. A good school encourages
youngsters to play and try things in as safe a setting as
possible, with good supervision. However, at least one staff
member at any preschool should be trained in first aid.

ACCIDENTS

If a child gets a small bruise or cut in school, the teachers
can usually deal with it. The same goes for a bellyache or
a headache. Your preschool should have first-aid materials
on hand, and school directors have usually been trained to
observe children closely for signs of illness. If there is a
resting room, a few minutes of "R and R" often fixes
things. However, if it's more significant than the usual cut
or scrape, the teacher or director should call you. For this
reason, the school should always know where to reach you
or another member of the family.

A parent told us, "I got a call from the teacher that my
child had slipped on the tile rim of a wading pool in the
park. She said he was resting and they were watching him
for signs of concussion. They'd already checked with the
school doctor. I was upset, but at least I felt they had done
all the right things immediately, such as calling me." In

this connection, you should tell the preschool whenever you're going to be away from your office or in a different place. Give them an alternative person to call if necessary. Make sure you have filled out a permission slip for emergency hospital medical attention.

SECURITY

These days everyone is concerned about children's security in school and out. Newspapers, TV broadcasts—even milk cartons—advertise the nightmare of children accosted, molested, or kidnapped. Certainly no one can minimize the increased peril of our times. Security measures in a preschool need to be strict and consistent, whether or not they are mandated by law. But which member of the triad should have the major responsibility for the security of a child? Parent? School? The children themselves?

HOW PARENTS CAN HELP

Parents need to think about ways in which they can enhance security for their children. First of all, you need to know what plans the school has in place for security and to cooperate with them. Obviously if you live in a high-crime area you'll want to see more thought given to the subject than if you live in the country. But wherever you live, you'll be more reassured if security systems are worked out. Some schools have locked doors to either the building or the preschool room. If a door is supposed to be locked when you leave, make sure it is locked. If you're given a key, take care of it. Don't give it to anyone else. You'll certainly have asked about security before you enrolled your child in a preschool. But sometimes you can see holes in the system after your child is there. If you are not happy with security arrangements, discuss the subject with the school. But keep in mind that the necessity for strict security varies from community to community. Make sure that your expectations and your own personal security measures for your child are appropriate for your neighborhood. One parent said he spoke up because he felt a little more caution was needed when a child was picked up at the end of the day. He thought there wasn't enough attention paid to who was leaving and with whom.

CAN PRESCHOOLERS PROTECT THEMSELVES?

How much responsibility for his own security can you put on a preschool child? Not too much. It's mainly up to you to see that the arrangements are in place. A note or a phone call to the school is a *must* if anyone other than the accustomed person is picking up your child at school. Some schools double-check by asking a child, "Justin, who is this?" when the person appears, making sure the child knows the person. As an additional precaution, even young children can understand a rule about not going anywhere with a stranger, but don't depend on them to act on it. Remember that two-, three-, and even four-year-olds can forget very easily. In order to make the stranger bugaboo strong enough to be unforgettable, you would probably have to make it so vivid that you might really scare your youngster.

Children in the early years are very literal. As an example, we offer the following story: Mom drummed into the head of four-year-old Todd that he was not to go home with anyone except her, unless he was told about the switch in advance. One day she asked Todd's dad at the last minute to do pickup, but forgot to tell Todd. So deeply had the security message sunk in that young Todd refused to get into the car with his own father!

Complicated warnings to young children may not stick,

or they may backfire, as this one did. Better to acknowledge that it is up to you and the school to do all the protecting until your child is old enough to participate in his own protection.

We asked teachers what they thought the preschool should tell children about protecting themselves from strangers. Most of them felt that it was not appropriate to lecture children on the subject, but that if the children brought it up, they helped to clarify the discussion with them. One teacher said, "In school we play a record called *I'm Too Smart for Strangers.* But other than that, we don't go into the subject. We don't think it's our job to bombard the kids with fear messages." But a teacher in another preschool said, "The children themselves bring up the subject, so sometimes we talk it over at Circle Time. I try to help them decide what to do."

PRESCHOOL LANGUAGE AND READING

Language activities are an important component of most preschool programs. One of the aims of the book corner and the dictated stories and charts is to foster literacy—in other words, to help children get ready to read and write and to give them a strong sense that reading and enjoyment go together.

No one knows for sure what age is the best one for beginning to teach reading—or even if there is a best age. Denmark teaches young people to read at age seven; Israel and Great Britain teach it at five; the United States, France, and Japan around age six. There's no evidence that any one of these timetables is better than the others or that children at one age learn better than at another.

What educators do know is that reading, like other skills of early childhood, seems to be acquired in stages. In spite

Children's pretend writing is one of the signs of print awareness.

of all the publicity about two-year-old readers, there is very little evidence that children learn to read in any lasting or meaningful way without having gone through some important and necessary steps first. Here's the way it usually happens:

As a baby, Jenny hears people talking. Gradually she sorts out those sounds into rhythmic patterns that she associates with people. *Mommy. Daddy.* Her own name— *Jenny.* She listens raptly as her parents and caregivers sing or read nursery rhymes to her or play games with her. At a certain age she begins to pick up important (to her) words. She can now appreciate a simple storybook with a plot, even though she may not understand all the language. Before Jenny learns to talk, she has a bank of language in her head that she understands, even if she can't yet say it. Once she begins to talk, she begins to call up the words she has already learned, and by hearing new words she adds to the storehouse. Meanwhile she sees other people reading and writing. At some point Jenny becomes aware that what her dad is saying as he reads her a bedtime story is connected with those squiggles on the page. She may pretend to write and read at this stage. Print awareness begins at around three for many children, particularly if they have grown up in a print-rich environment. On their own they begin to spell their own names, to recognize other letters, and to be aware that words are the things between the white spaces on a page. At this stage or later some children catch on to the fact that you look at words from left to right and from top to bottom. This is a very important part of getting ready to read.

In Jenny's case, her print awareness increases dramatically from age three to five. She begins to notice words on restrooms, in gas stations. ''Exit,'' she shouts proudly each time she sees the sign.

Jenny's development of print awareness is pretty typical. In a recent test of 229 children ages four, five, and six, more than 50 percent could recognize a word presented in its familiar context (for example, *stop,* in the familiar stop-sign shape). But the same words seen outside their surrounding environment were less frequently identified. All of which tells us that reading is a skill that comes at least partly out of experiences in the normal course of children's lives. In other words, the ''lessons'' are all around. Children want to know what those signs say. They want to be able to read those books that can tell them something about a picture that has caught their eye. They *want* to recognize their own names and those of their friends.

What should preschool contribute to a child's getting ready to read? And how do you know if your child's preschool is doing too much or too little?

In a teacher-centered, B-type program, your child is likely to bring home evidence that there's work being done on letters and numbers, printing, word recognition, and other very specific tasks. She may be part of a preprimer reading program or a reading-readiness program. But there are problems with this approach. For one thing, many children (particularly boys) have neither the small-motor coordination to be doing pencil-and-paper drills nor the readiness to sit and attend to activities that essentially belong to first grade. Some youngsters will be restless or act up if they are forced to concentrate on tasks that have little developmental appropriateness for them. Or a child may get bored, in which case learning to read later on is likely to become distasteful and a grind rather than a joyful discovery at the optimum time.

It is extremely important for parents to know what's going on vis-à-vis reading. You should make sure that your child is not being turned off to reading in preschool by being pushed to ''Go'' when he should be at ''Get Ready.''

In a preschool or child care center where teachers have their eye on each child's individual development, children have print all around them and they learn about it each day. There are labels, charts, names everywhere, but no one necessarily makes a lesson of these things. Instead, they're there for the children to use as a way of tuning up their eyes and ears.

The teacher may take dictation of their stories and then read them back to them. They see their own names and the names of their friends posted in prominent places. They are read stories and they may "read" wordless picture books to the other children. They help keep simple records, follow recipes when doing a cooking project, and play games that involve shape, size, and sequence, all of which are language skills.

Here's one example of this process that happened at a child care center:

Two four-year-olds were drawing. One said, "I'm going to sign my name to this picture."

The other said, "I want to sign my name, too. But I don't know how."

The first child then said, "I'll show you how to do it."

She took her friend by the hand and brought her over to the cubbies. "You can copy your name from here," she said. What a great discovery! And what a nice sharing of information.

But while having books and print as part of an environment will make for future readers, there are even broader and deeper meanings to the language connection. Recently there has been a new focus on what educators call Whole Language. Whole Language is a way of teaching prereading, reading, and other language skills through all the processes that involve language—writing, talking, listening to stories, creating stories, artwork, and dramatic play as well as through more traditional pathways. While Whole Language is primarily a philosophy of teaching in the primary grades, its implications are filtering down to preschool programs. Seen in this context, show-and-tell, reading stories, writing (dictating) original stories, and dramatic play are all part of a Whole Language experience in the good preschool setting.

How Parents Can Help

No one has to tell a parent that reading opens the door to all the other basic skills. But experience with language in all its forms opens the door to reading. What can a parent do at home to sponsor the kinds of experiences that lead to learning to read? Perhaps the best approach is to keep reading to your children and to keep handy for preschoolers a variety of simple materials and/or games and other language-connected things that will stimulate their natural curiosity. "Activity books" may be among them, as long as the simple tasks called for are not too hard or practiced for too long a time (fifteen minutes of an activity book is plenty). Rebus books are great for prereading, and you will find the rebus idea used widely in good preschools. It can be adapted in many ways. For example, one school we visited had the word *truck* as well as a picture of the truck above the bin where the toy trucks were kept. This picture-plus-word device was repeated for many of the supplies. What it did was to make available for the children an easy way of recognizing the proper place for things. At the same time it offered a chance to get to know the configuration of the word for objects they could already name.

You can exchange notes and make simple signs at home. One-word notes are fun for children to decode. *Cookies* propped against the cookie jar tells a child to help himself. *Teeth* leaning casually on the soap dish reminds him to brush. A trip to the supermarket can be a richer experience if a parent is willing to involve a preschooler in finding words, signs, and numbers.

Why is this a better way to learn to read than a prereading "skills" program? Because, like the word *stop* in the shape of a stop sign, it's a form of reading context, and because it stimulates reading when the child is ready, not when the adult is ready.

THE EARLY READER

A parent says, ''My child is four and she's reading. Won't she be bored in kindergarten?''

Occasionally, and it's pretty rare, a youngster will get the hang of reading before kindergarten. We're not talking here about the child who has grown up on flash cards and prompts or who has memorized a story so completely it seems as if she is reading. We mean a child who actually knows how to decode print. Early readers occasionally seem to develop overnight. They are invariably children who have such a keen interest in the printed word that they teach themselves to read rather than waiting for a grown-up to come along and teach it to them or read it for them. The key element with these children seems to be desire—which should tell us all something about the teaching of reading.

What does the reading preschooler do in a developmental preschool? The answer is—plenty. Often they are the very things that an early reader may need practice in, such as large-motor coordination. Parents often worry a great deal about a child being bored in kindergarten if he or she already knows how to read at four or five. But what's boring to a grown-up is not necessarily boring to a child. Children like to recap what they already know. If you don't believe it, watch an older sibling horn in on younger brother's puzzle or game book. ''That's too young for you,'' we say, when what we should be saying is, ''What a clever way to practice what you already know and get it fixed in your head!''

Don't assume that boredom in preschool or later in kindergarten necessarily comes with early reading. For one thing, the thrust of a good preschool is to develop a whole preschooler, not a creature called "the early reader." A good preschool program will have an endless world of social and physical as well as more narrowly defined learning experiences for any child—whether early in reading skills or in sports skills, for that matter. When your early reader is ready for kindergarten, you can discuss with the new teacher what her plans are for the year. If she knows there is a reader in her group, she may be able to use him or her as a mentor for other children. This will both reinforce the reader and inspire the nonreaders in the group. One teacher we know encouraged a young bookworm to try his hand at drawing while the others were struggling with the letters he already knew. He did a great job of illustrating some of the stories he read and developed a skill that increased his general competence and maturity.

No child, reader or nonreader, needs to be bored in a good preschool with a good teacher. But you and the teacher should certainly talk about ways and means of rounding out your early reader's preschool experience. If there seems to be no room later in public school for a little accommodation, you'll have to ask for a conference and insist that some thought be given to your youngster's individual needs.

Cultural Diversity

One of the things we've already mentioned is that an ideal preschool program has children from different cultural, racial, and socioeconomic backgrounds. In some neighborhoods, of course, this is more possible than in others. In my own particular suburb in northeastern Pennsylvania, poor children and middle-class children may both go to the same preschool, but they come from similar racial and ethnic backgrounds. In more metropolitan neighborhoods, there may be more of an ethnic mix, but less of a socioeconomic one. In any case, the ideal is variety, and many good preschool programs make a special effort through busing, scholarships, or their selection processes to attain a melting-pot atmosphere.

There are some sound reasons why a good developmental preschool program tries to have cultural diversity. Children of different races, religions, and economic and cultural backgrounds have something to give one another. They can share customs, experiences, vocabulary, and ways of being and doing that enrich all preschoolers. Children share their culture just by being together, and good preschool teachers help to enhance the sharing so that the children gain in self-esteem.

Here's one way in which this kind of learning can happen among a group of four- and five-year-olds in the Bank Street School for Children: A parent may come in wearing a scarf in a unique way. The children may notice. So the teacher starts a discussion about scarves. She may say, "How do they use scarves in your family?"

Since there is much cultural diversity in the class, the children discover that

Scarves come in different colors, shapes, and fabrics.

A scarf can be used as a head covering.

It can be used as a bag for groceries.

You can wear it around your neck, your waist, your hips.

You can wrap it all sorts of ways.

You can carry a baby in a scarf, worn as a "snuggly."

Both boys and girls can wear scarves.

Once having been made aware of scarves, the children may bring in pictures from *National Geographic* or other sources that show scarves used in a new or unusual way. They may begin a list or a folder or connect their scarf "research" with art. They bring in their scarves and try different ways of wrapping and wearing them. Meanwhile, they are learning that their family may not use the scarf for the same purpose another family does but that a different way is equally valid. This expands children's own possibilities and interests in areas that go beyond the scarf discussion. At the same time it gives them a valuable international perspective that will help them now and later to function better in a diverse world.

How Parents Can Help

Parents can help their children gain pride in their own background and appreciation for other cultures. One way is to support the school's efforts in this direction. Take an active part in recruiting parents and children from a variety of cultures. Encourage friendships between your child and children from other backgrounds and cultures. It's one thing to see people who look different and act different from you on TV. But if we know that children learn from concrete experiences, then seeing and talking with many different kinds of people, adults as well as children, has to be meaningful. And if you can possibly find the time, share your own culture personally with the school. Teachers can't be experts in every culture, and a good preschool particularly welcomes this kind of special sharing. You might volunteer to read a book in your own language (children love this even if they don't understand it) or cook a special dish or simply add a few props to the dramatic play area. If you don't have time to come to school yourself, you might share some photographs or a family artifact that your child can explain. These contributions will give pride to both you and your child.

A NONSEXIST EDUCATION

Boys and girls find their role identification wherever they spend time. If preschool is a big part of their days and weeks, it will follow that school will have an influence on how youngsters think of their femininity or masculinity. That's why it is so important for parents to look at whether preschool is encouraging both boys and girls to develop in all ways or whether it is reinforcing old stereotypes.

In the best of all possible settings, there would be male as well as female staff. These on-site males would provide healthy role models and give children an added sense of the male as nurturer. If you find a preschool with some male teachers or aides, consider it a plus. In a good preschool or child care center, boys and girls participate equally in all activities. Boys are busy in the cooking corner, girls build with blocks and climb up the monkey bars. There's no ''Girls don't do that'' or ''That's not for boys; only sissies do that.'' Books, blocks, dolls, housekeeping corner—all reflect equality. Even language is liberated from sexism; the fireman becomes the firefighter.

In the same way, boys are not automatically assumed to be the roughnecks or bullies. Girls are not expected always to be good or to keep their clothes clean. You'll notice that the teachers don't have separate voices for girls and boys and that they don't seem to favor one sex over the other.

However, in the most equal preschool, you may observe that girls gravitate to certain activities and boys to others. One teacher says that in her group the boys are usually more fond of the block corner and the girls of the coloring markers. Whether this reflects innate differences or exposure, we don't know. The point is that kids should be able to make free choices and not be pushed into what are regarded as gender-related activities.

How Parents Can Help

If you value nonsexist learning, you can help extend it at home. In fact, you may be doing just that if you and your husband or other partner share household tasks as well as the financial responsibilities of the family. If you have an interesting job that's an unusual one for a women, or for a man, you may be asked to share your experiences with the youngsters in school.

The most important thing you can do is to expose your children to the fullest possibilities of their gender, be it masculine or feminine. You might even want to get some books from the library that speak to this theme, such as *William's Doll,* by Charlotte Zolotow (Harper & Row), or *Mothers Can Do Anything,* by Joe Lasker (Albert Whitman).

EVERYDAY PRESCHOOL ROUTINES

—

CLOTHES AND DRESSING

Clothing plays a part in daily preschool (and later school) life. Many centers send home a list of what they like children to wear. It is based on experience and has sensible reasons behind it. For instance, since preschoolers are taken to the bathroom frequently, the school will suggest clothes that can slip on and off easily. Pants with elastic tops are good for both sexes for this reason. Overalls with a fly-front closing may work for boys who are ready to use the toilet standing up. Proper footwear is important, too. Sturdy shoes with rubber soles give a grip on the vinyl floors that are typical in nursery and other preschools. Sneakers are the one item that seems to be part of the uniform dress code of preschool, at least according to the kids. Sneakers are fine, but they should be good ones if they're going to be worn every day. Dr. Joseph Dobrusin, a podiatrist who is in favor of sneakers for both children and adults, says that cheap sneakers are no bargain for a child's feet. Shop for them as you'd shop for quality shoes and expect to pay as much.

Snow and rain boots that open wide and have do-it-yourself fasteners are good. Just make sure they are roomy enough so that there's no yank and struggle. Sweaters and jackets that go on by putting the arms through are better than over-the-head garments. Snaps or Velcro closings are easier than buttons. Toggles are fun, but they're hard for some kids to manage. Small zippers are difficult for small fingers, so if something has a zipper, it should be a big one. Hoods have an advantage over hats since they're attached and won't get lost. Mittens are better than gloves because they keep hands warmer and are easier to slip on. Clip-ons for both gloves and mittens are a good idea since they keep them attached to jackets. As for shirts and blouses, the ones with comfortably wide neck openings or front openings are usually more desirable.

Certain clothing concerns are regional; for example, in the Northeast, teachers may be pretty specific about the kinds of boots they prefer children to wear. In Florida or Arizona, preschool teachers don't have the chore of putting on dozens of pairs of boots, but they may insist (and rightly so) that children bring hats or sunglasses as protection from the sun when they play outside. Umbrellas tend to get lost in all fifty states, and most of them are hard for young children to handle; they can also be dangerous. A wide-brimmed hat and raincoat or a poncho with a hood is a better choice. Most schools will ask for a change of clothes to be left at school in case of a spill or other accident.

So far we've talked mainly about teacher and parent. But it's important that a child have some say over what he or she wears to preschool. Children become conscious of what they wear at very young ages these days. Sometimes it's a duck on a shirt or a coat of many colors. More and more, it's a style or fad that even the youngest tot knows about. In many families pretty or stylish clothes are admired and made much of, and children learn to like and enjoy nice things and new things. There's nothing wrong with a little fad and fashion as long as it doesn't get in the way of other things at preschool. But if what Jill wore to school or the kind of sneakers Aaron has becomes a constant subject for discussion, comparison, and envy, then perhaps clothes have assumed too much importance in preschool life and everyone has to deemphasize them.

How Parents Can Help

It is up to parents to decide how much autonomy a preschooler has in choosing his clothing for school. Sometimes a child will fasten on one item of clothing for going to preschool. A baseball cap, a certain pair of suspenders, or a certain hair barrette becomes a sort of amulet, and a child wouldn't dream of going to the center without wearing it. I remember one of my sons had a Davy Crockett fur hat that he wore for months (winter and summer!). These are harmless clothes fetishes, and while the item can wind up looking pretty disreputable, it's important for a child to be able to wear this thing he or she has picked, especially as it gives the wearer a sort of imagined protective armor and sense of security.

But what do you do if your son insists on wearing his shirt inside out or if your daughter wants to wear her newest party dress and white shoes to school when you know she is going to ruin them playing in the sandbox? In this case, *appropriate* is the key word. You may have to get her interested in wearing something else. At the same time, it may be important for that boy to wear his shirt inside out because he put it on that way or for that girl to feel special by wearing something she doesn't usually wear to school, such as a dress.

Make sure that preschool is not reinforcing a great deal of emphasis on clothes. Sometimes a well-meaning teacher will make too much of what one child is wearing. Your child may pick up on that message, especially if it is delivered often.

Parents have different views on what kids should wear. Some mothers and dads like a child to go to preschool dressed up, because they regard it as a special place rather than a play setting. This is a matter of personal taste and cultural background. The only thing is, if your insistence that your girl wear a dress or your boy a shirt and tie interferes with his or her ability to join the other children in painting and water-table play, or in the tumble of outdoor activity, then you're not helping either of them make the most of their time in preschool. In addition, you have to decide whether you'll be comfortable if your child comes home with clay on his tie, paint on his shirt, and dirt on his jacket. Most parents decide after a few weeks that simple, comfortable, washable clothing is easier on everyone.

FOOD

There is a good reason why some of our most vivid childhood memories revolve around food. It is clear that food has deep meanings, both for parents and for children. In preschools it's one of the first things parents ask about, and they continue to want to know if a child is eating and what he or she is eating in preschool.

Food is an important part of the preschool program. A good deal of thought is given to both its preparation and its presentation. There's more and more emphasis on healthy foods served with an eye to color, texture, and nutritional balance. There's a move away from fats and sweets. Even in half-day nursery school, snacks are

Cooking integrates many kinds of learning in the early childhood setting.

thoughtfully planned; these days you're much more apt to find crackers, cheese, raisins, and fruits being offered than cookies or fried chips.

Preschools know, too, that children can get set in their food ways. That's why they try to serve a variety of foods that may introduce them to new taste sensations. Often these foods also give them a glimpse into another culture. In that way they broaden their horizons while educating their taste buds.

Talk around the table is a wonderful way to share all kinds of pleasures as well as the one of eating. Often it can introduce children to new words as well as to new tastes. Rice and beans become a nice change from hamburger and potatoes. Chinese noodles are a little different from, but as acceptable as, spaghetti. Vegetables are sometimes relished when they're presented raw as finger food, and exotic fruits for dessert can provide an endless lesson in "naming and knowing."

Food in fact provides nourishment in many ways in the preschool program. Food talk comes up all the time in preschool, both at mealtime and at other times during the day. Plastic representations of food are sometimes part of the Housekeeping Corner, and puzzles in the shape of foods help young children learn all kinds of concepts (shape, sequence, counting), as well as the names of fruits and vegetables.

But perhaps one of the favorite ways of integrating food into preschool is through cooking. Children of both sexes seem to enjoy making simple dishes—butter, fruit salad, scrambled eggs, popcorn. And through the process children learn many things.

They learn number concepts:

"Let's put in *two* cups of milk, and *one* teaspoon of honey."

or

"Let's see *how many* pieces of apple we have cut up."

They learn sequence:

"*First* we cut up the fruit, *next* we add the honey. *Then* we ..."

They can even learn a little science:

"What do you think made the cream turn to butter?"
"What happened when we baked the cookies?"

Cooking and food preparation are real-life learning. When children cook in preschool, they also help to lay out the ingredients and clean up afterward. All of this helps prepare both boys and girls to do their share at home in the family. It goes without saying that mealtimes at home and at school should be pleasant, shared times. In preschool they tend to be, because most teachers do not feel it's desirable to urge children to eat.

Sometimes youngsters will pass up something new that they don't recognize or simply say, "I hate this." But most children not only eat pretty well in school, they do get around to trying new things, especially if they see other children doing it. In fact, many children eat better in preschool than at home exactly because there is no pressure on them about eating. It's good for kids to experiment with new foods. It's part of independence and should be encouraged. On the other hand, children do get food phobias and will go through a period of eating one thing, such as a hamburger. Preschools usually ignore these fads, and eventually the child returns to a more-or-less balanced diet.

How Parents Can Help

Relax. Once you make sure that the school has a good dietitian/cook and clean facilities for preparing food, you can usually cross food off your worry list. The only exceptions are in cases where a child has an allergy or some other medical problem. If your child needs a special diet, you'll have to discuss that with the school. If your family has special requirements, such as being vegetarians or eating only kosher food, you should talk it over. One day care center director told us that she found a largely vegetarian diet not only accommodated the vegetarians and religious nonmeat eaters but could also easily be made to square with good nutrition practices.

One thing you may want to do is to find out some of the reasoning behind the choice of foods that are served in your preschool. For example, in some preschool child care centers, a breakfast corner is set up for the children who may not have had breakfast. Research has shown that in some families breakfast is a thing of the past. At the same time, the Iowa breakfast studies showed that physical and mental functions of children were better when they had breakfast. More recent studies go even further. They indicate that older children may actually perform tasks such as beginning reading and math better in the morning after a good feed. So if your school doesn't have a breakfast corner, maybe you can adapt the idea at home. Lay out cereals or whole-grain muffins and spread, milk, and juice, along with utensils, so that your youngster can help herself, buffet style.

If your child is a one-menu youngster, you can't expect the school to continue that policy. We know one family whose child ate bananas and little else. When the child went to preschool, her parents were sure she would starve. But after a short hunger strike, the banana eater branched out. After that her parents were able to enlarge her menu at home.

What happens when children bring their own lunches to school? Often schools distribute guidelines about food, so that no child will be bringing gooey cupcakes in violation of the school's general feelings about sweets. Still, even with guidelines, family food patterns are bound to show up in the lunch box. This, too, can be a learning experience for everyone. Lots can be learned when the child with the artichokes vinaigrette sits next to the kid with the baloney sandwich. Two-year-olds generally stay with their own lunches, but as children get older, they will often talk about the contents of their friends' lunch boxes. Sometimes they may swap lunches, although some preschools don't permit this.

It is inevitable that some clash of tastes is going to surface if everyone is doing his own food thing. If you're a vegetarian family, for example, your child may get his first contraband liverwurst sandwich in preschool. This is something you'll have to handle as a family; it's not something you can expect the school to monitor.

My friend Joel had a pretty inventive solution to the vegetarian-versus-others question. His eight-year-old son, Morgan, was going on a fishing trip with his Cub Scout troop, and they were planning to eat the fish they caught. Since the family does not eat "flesh," Joel baked Morgan some cheese biscuits in the shape of fish. That way Morgan could maintain his principles yet be one of the group!

If you're against sweets and other children are bringing cookies and puddings in their lunch boxes, you're liable to get some four-year-old flak. You'll have to decide what you want to do about it. Possibly now is one of the times to say, "That's what they eat in their house. But in our house we eat this."

It is very hard for parents not to be involved in their children's food intake. Some schools will put leftovers back into lunch boxes so parents will know what has been eaten, because "Did you eat all your lunch in school?" is such an often-asked question.

Try to keep food from becoming an issue, either at home or at school. If you feel strongly about some aspect of the lunch program, it may be a good idea to have a parent meeting on the subject (with coffee and sandwiches after!).

PHYSICAL PLAY

With all the emphasis on honing mental skills, something has been overlooked that was formerly the domain of childhood. Plain, old-fashioned running around—physical exercise. Nowadays, between TV and car and bus travel, some preschoolers don't get too much chance to move around. They're overfed and underexercised, and it often shows. The father of the three-year-old may be out jogging every morning, and Mom may go to aerobics in the evening, but the younger member of the family may be sitting at his electronic letters game, breeding fat cells.

Many physicians are alarmed at the way in which young children's bodies are being neglected while their brains are being exercised beyond bounds. Dr. Mark Levine of the National Institute of Health says fat cells form in young bodies before the age of three. Overfed, underexercised children form more and larger fat cells, and these are harder to get rid of later. That's why finding a preschool with a good outdoor/physical play program is important. Children need running-around time. They need a place to work off high spirits and excess energy. "Use your outside voice outside," a teacher tells a boisterous four-year-old. Kids need to use their "outside voices" and muscles.

Preschools approach exercise in a number of different ways. At one preschool they have a well-equipped playground. At another they have a rooftop play space with room to run around. At a third they have a nearby park with safe, soft surfaces under the swings and monkey bars, and they take the all-day preschoolers there twice a day when the weather is nice. At Kindercare centers, as we mentioned, they have excellent outdoor space and equipment of all kinds.

In Bank Street's Lower School, there's an exercise/

movement class in addition to the outdoor rooftop playground. The movement instructor, Roberta Altman, has youngsters as young as three walking the balance beam, moving hand over hand on a climbing gym, tumbling on mats, and generally gaining control of their bodies. Ms. Altman integrates body language with other kinds of language learning. There's a short session of talk after each class, in which children describe what they did on the equipment or talk about what they plan to do next time. Sometimes a child is encouraged to use the exercise equipment in a new or extended way. In one such recent class, Ms. Altman said to a youngster, "Dan, how did you manage to do that special hand grip on the bars?" The youngster, clearly pleased at being noticed, said, "I just thought it out today."

Indeed, exercise is not only physical but mental. Under the direction of a trained teacher it has limitless extensions and opportunities for learning geared to the developmental needs of the child. For example, in the Bank Street movement class an unusually energetic youngster was encouraged to use the balance beam, where he had to slow down a bit and use control over his body in order to walk the beam. A quieter child was lured into somersaults on the barrel, which was a daring activity for her. In movement class, concepts of space are constantly being explored. Children get to understand high, low, and medium in a very organic way. They get the feel of controlling their bodies in space. This is very important preparation for a host of later physical activities—dancing, competitive games, team sports.

As a professional with years of experience, Roberta Altman also has some definite ideas of what are appropriate physical games for young children. She says, "Children two to five don't play competitive games well. They're too young to understand winning and losing. They can't be good sports because they still get frustrated too easily. And if they're forced into competition, they get very rigid and can't do their best. So we emphasize games where they do what they can and where everyone can come out a winner in some way. We may play tag, where no one person really loses. We'll talk about the game afterward and analyze the strategies that people used to tag or to escape being tagged. In other words, we're getting them ready to compete well later. But first they learn to play together well and to appreciate one another. Gradually they learn to 'referee' disputes among themselves, which is the basis of sportsmanship. Meanwhile they're learning to use their bodies in more precise ways. Then, and only then, are they ready for competition.''

How Parents Can Help

Don't undervalue the importance of outdoor play and exercise. First of all, make sure the preschool is providing the physical program it promised. It doesn't have to be organized; just running around or rolling down a grassy hillside is fun and far better than exercise *lessons* if they are simply miniversions of adult classes. Movement and exercise, like other parts of the program, should be geared to the child's age and stage. This is a good rule outside of preschool as well. Most sports professionals who know young children will urge parents not to push youngsters into competitive and/or team sports before age seven or eight. Their bodies are not ready for the precise movements that many sports require, and they can't handle the discipline required to train or the frustration of not winning or doing well. (In fact, it is for these reasons that the New York City Ballet won't accept young dancers before eight or nine.)

Make sure that your child is dressed in suitable clothes for exercise or outdoor activities at preschool. If there's any reason why your youngster's participation in exercise should be limited, let the school know right away.

TOILETING

The bathroom and toileting enter preschool with your youngster. To begin with, if a youngster isn't out of diapers yet, some preschools won't take him. The reason is that preschools have to have different facilities if they care for children still in diapers. Often there are different health code requirements. It is altogether easier to administer a preschool where bathroom is a do-it-yourself activity.

Unfortunately, this policy doesn't do much for a child who is a little late-into-bloomers. The result is that the parent of a two-and-a-half-year-old who wants to start the child in preschool may be tempted to give an extra push toward toilet training. If a child is ready to be trained anyway, a little extra effort in that direction may work. But sometimes the push can actually slow things down.

It is usually not a good idea to make a special effort at toilet training just to get into a certain preschool. It puts needless pressure on you and on your youngster. Besides, the new skill on the toilet may disappear when he starts preschool. It might be better either to look for a setting that has facilities for diapering or to wait until your youngster learns to use the bathroom at home. In fact, toilet training is one of the controls that often goes haywire when a child starts school, even if it was in place before.

Sometimes it's separation anxiety that works on bladder and bowel (see chapter 5). Children show their feelings in different ways. This may be the way your child says, "Being away from home has got me kind of upset." If it is separation anxiety, time will probably cure it. Teachers are very used to this sort of thing and know how to handle it.

Sometimes toilet slips can be traced to something specific. Look for simple explanations before you start worrying. For example, one parent mentioned that her son had a problem with the zipper on his pants and consequently had an "accident" in preschool. Another parent said that for some reason, her four-year-old was afraid to use the toilet at school because it had a seat with a space in front. Because of this fear, he soiled his pants and felt bad about it. But he didn't tell anyone his fears for quite some time.

Toilet training may be a temporary casualty of preschool, but in the long run much more is learned about bathroom practices than is lost. Children of both sexes become comfortable with toilet routines through seeing other children and sharing information in a casual way. In a good preschool, teachers help children become self-sufficient in the bathroom without blaming or punishing. Children are toileted several times during a morning and a teacher always keeps her eyes open for the youngster who has to go and is waiting too long or the one who has just learned control and needs to be helped. Many children who have been using a potty seat at home graduate to a regular toilet in preschool. Boys may learn to urinate standing up by watching other boys. Girls and boys learn bathroom routines such as wiping themselves and washing their hands.

Many children who are not too far away from their diapering days are often extremely generous about encouraging other children in toilet habits. Children who see other children sitting on a toilet are less afraid of that big gaping hole.

HOW PARENTS CAN HELP

First of all, you need to share with the preschool just where your child is as far as toileting is concerned. If your son is just out of diapers, say so. Then the school can anticipate accidents and help him toward full control. If your daughter will use the bathroom to urinate but still has bowel movements off in a corner somewhere, communicate this fact. If your child is fully trained but still uses a potty seat, say so. Some preschools don't have potty seats, and this could be a problem for her. One teacher told us that she had a youngster having toilet problems for seven weeks before she discovered that the child was used to a potty seat at home.

So share with the preschool everything you think will be helpful regarding your child's toilet routine. Dress your youngster in clothes that make it easier to use the toilet without help. Tell the teacher whether he is used to having someone go to the bathroom with him or prefers to go alone. Always tell the school if there's any chronic problem (such as constipation). Send extra clothing if you think your child will need a change It may seem less than lofty philosophy, but the truth is, a child can only be comfortable and free to get the most out of preschool if he or she is relaxed about the bathroom.

SHOW-AND-TELL

Some preschools call it Sharing Time. Others call it Circle Time, because often the children sit in a circle for this activity. Whatever you call it, show-and-tell is very much part of almost every preschool curriculum, and part of many kindergarten programs as well.

The main purpose of show-and-tell is for children to share talk, ideas, a special toy or book, or experiences. A teacher usually sets aside a time or a day and asks the children in the group to bring in some object or idea that interests them. (At some centers children learn the day of the week by the fact that it's show-and-tell day.)

The children take turns presenting their photo or toy, or the leaf that they found on their trip to the country. Other children chime in and ask questions or in other ways add to the talk fest. The teacher is there to guide the discussion, but at its best the kids often run show-and-tell pretty much on their own. There's a great deal of learning that can come out of these weekly exchanges. Children learn to express feelings and ideas and to share them with other children. They get a glimpse into other children's lives and learn about other families and their experiences in a way that is enriching for both the talker and the listener.

For example, on a recent show-and-tell day at Children's Underground, Nubia brought in a picture of her grandmother who is one hundred years old. The children were fascinated and asked lots of questions. There was much speculation about what it's like to be old. Another child brought in a record that he liked and played it, while a third child shared with the class the experience of going to buy a pumpkin in the country—with an actual pumpkin in tow as evidence of the event.

How Parents Can Help

As a parent, you may be recruited into the show-and-tell "act." Your son or daughter will ask you (usually at the last minute) to help choose something to bring to preschool. It's important for you to know that show-and-tell is basically time for sharing something special to your child, but not necessarily something material—or something in any way precious from an adult point of view. If she does bring an object, it should be one that has some sort of special meaning for her. A book or record often has that special quality, as does a beautifully colored fall leaf or a shell picked up on the beach.

A child sometimes has a little trouble figuring out the kind of item that's suitable for show-and-tell. He may not realize that you don't have to buy something to bring and that the rock with the fossil in it that he found is a good choice. Mom and Dad can be helpful by talking about show-and-tell in advance so that a child will have plenty of time to make up his mind. If he seems at a loss, you might make a few suggestions. One of the many learning perks of show-and-tell is the process of making the choice of what to bring. You don't want to take that away from your child, but you may be able to offer a little support and guidance.

Show-and-tell is a valuable part of preschool. All kinds of learning come out of it, including the ability to speak up, to say why you like something, to have opinions, and to make critical choices.

CHILD-TO-CHILD

A good preschool knows that children learn from one another. So you may find that while the teachers are well aware of your child's individual needs each day, many activities are done in groups. A certain amount of importance is attached to the social business of being with other children and interacting with them.

"Isn't this a little forced?" you may wonder. "My social life wasn't so consciously arranged when I was their age.''

Sure, things used to be different. When I was growing up, there were neighborhoods where youngsters of the same and even different ages played together. And there were big families, who made their own neighborhoods. Nowadays both the big family and the easy street socializing of young children is, in many places, gone. If it exists at all, it is only in little pockets of suburbia or exurbia where it's safe for young children to be outside together. Many people live in high rises where kids meet only in elevators or in suburbs where it's often not considered safe for a child to be outside unsupervised and where few parents have time for such all-day supervision. These days it requires real effort on the part of a parent or caregiver to get a child together with another child of any age. This is not so much a promotion for mixed-age grouping in preschool as it is a reminder that in some places children have limited opportunities to meet other children of any age, and particularly children who are different from them in any way.

There's no way to properly measure what children get from one another. To have someone to play with is only the beginning. There's a whole raft of skills that kids pick up from other kids—from how to tie shoelaces to how to tell a story out loud to how to climb the monkey bars or how to go to the bathroom. Occasionally they copy behavior you'd just as soon they hadn't copied. But on balance the good far outweighs the bad.

One of the aspects worth mentioning about preschool is the opportunity it offers for children to interact with both older and younger children in a safe, constructive way. In a good preschool older and younger kids get together for

213

certain activities. Good teachers use the older kids as
models for the younger and may even, at times, plan activities that give older children a chance to help younger ones.
At Montessori centers, children of three, four, and five are
deliberately put in one room together. Older children teach
younger ones and at the same time get a chance to recap
what they've learned. At the Phelps Child Care Center,
older children are deliberately taken to see and play with
younger children. Given the fact that most public schools
are arranged by grade (and never the grades shall meet),
if your youngster is an only child, preschool may be his
one opportunity to meet and play with both older and
younger children.

How Parents Can Help

Support the idea of mixed-age groups, or at least groups
that interact. If your child's preschool is arranged by age
groups, find out whether they ever get together. If they
don't, suggest it as an idea. If your child doesn't get to
mix with older and younger children, think about enlisting
an older (trusted) child as a sometime companion and
mentor and paying an occasional visit to a younger child.

One of the nicest social aspects of preschool is the easy
and spontaneous afterschool friendships that often spring
up between children. ''Can he (she) come to my house
after school?'' is a question mothers and fathers often hear
at pickup or delivery time. It's a good question, and shows
that your youngster is bringing home some of the social
lessons of preschool. Afterschool visits are valuable in
many ways, over and above the fact that it's purely fun to
have someone to play with one-on-one. Sometimes they're
a ''first'' for a child in terms of being willing to go to an
unfamiliar home. A shy child may be encouraged to
broaden his horizons by going to the home of someone he

knows from school and see how someone else's family is. And the only child can learn something about sharing from his school buddy who comes to visit.

Parents should try to create chances for kids to get together once in a while after school or on weekends if (and only if) it's not a major hassle for you and if it's something the children want. If your child goes to preschool for a half day and if she's dying to have Monica come home with her, then fine. If, on the other hand, your child goes to a child care center until six, you might think twice about having Monica come for supper. Your child may need your company or a little privacy more than she needs Monica. You might rather have Monica come on a Saturday or a holiday during the day, when both children will be less tired. Plan these visits in advance and feel free to cancel if your child isn't up to par or changes her mind. And don't feel that you have to make a date for your youngster for every day in the week, even though he suddenly seems to want to be with his buddies every minute.

Keep the visit short the first time. Sometimes a child will be willing to go to a friend's house but not to stay for a meal. Respect this; don't push either your own child or the friend into more sociability than she's ready for. A good rule is to keep your arrangements loose and always make sure that both children are in favor of getting together. In other words, you can encourage it, but it should be the child's choice.

A conversation I recently overheard between two fathers and their children at Bank Street seemed to illustrate this partnership aspect of making dates with young children. One father said to the other, "I understand our boys are supposed to get together on Wednesday. But we can't bring Eric over to your house as we had planned. So can Don come to our place instead?" The second father turned to his son and asked, "Is that all right with you if you go to Eric's house instead of his coming to our house?" The four-year-old thought very carefully. Then he said, "Okay."

It was good that his father asked him, instead of simply making the arrangement. In fact, Don may have been ready to have Eric to his place but not yet ready to travel. Socializing is one way to extend the social lessons of preschool. Parents, too, can enjoy social benefits. Often the parents of your child's best friend are people you become close to.

ELECTRONIC LEARNING

COMPUTERS

In some quarters computers are still being heralded as the answer to early learning (although it's not quite clear what the question is). Some preschools have installed computers, usually at the request of parents. When you are preschool shopping, it is easy to be seduced by an array of handsome computer hardware. However, it would be a mistake to choose a preschool on the basis of its having or not having a computer. Although computers can be used as an educational tool, especially for older children, there is more to the story.

The best thing about computers is the fact that they are interactive. They ask the user to do something. They can get children to think. The worst thing about them is that many software programs, especially for preschoolers, are no more than silly drills that teach skills better learned in other ways than sitting at a monitor. Many pediatricians feel that those dancing pixels are not the best thing for the eyes of young children. When you consider that computer monitor viewing must be added to the time a child already spends watching television, you have to conclude that pre-school computing is dispensable.

TV AND VCR

Video cassette recorders are the latest add-on in some pre-schools. Like the television set, the VCR is essentially a passive machine. One supervisor of child care centers summed it up by saying flatly that she couldn't think of a single reason why a VCR should be in a preschool center. Most preschool directors don't consider VCRs basic equip-ment for their settings. These gadgets seem to go against the educational grain of early childhood teachers, and for some good reasons. Good preschool teachers like children to be doing things in preschool rather than having passive experiences that turn them into "couch potatoes."

Television is a little different story. Even though there's no TV set in most preschools, the tube does go to school. Just listen to a group of preschoolers in dramatic play:

Marisa: "I must be Big Bird."

Donald: "No, no. I must be Big Bird. You must be Kermit. And I say ..."

A new child coming into this group can join the play as soon as she picks up on the conversation. Even if she doesn't know the children, she knows Kermit and Big Bird. Ellen Galinsky, who writes and does research on working families, points out that TV has become a kind of social cement that bonds children together through shared visuals. That is a positive side of "the box," and one that parents can help foster. If TV is watched selectively, it can be both a learning experience and another way for a youngster to join his peer group.

On the other hand, young children just aren't capable of sifting the many messages of video. They are influenced by commercials, as every parent knows; and if they watch a steady diet of action-adventure and violence, they will be affected by it. According to Dr. Jerome Singer, of Yale University, in the latest studies conducted both here and in other countries it was found that young children who were heavy watchers of violent TV were more likely to be aggressive and restless later on in middle childhood.

PARENTS AND PRESCHOOL TECHNOLOGY

Computers neither make nor break a preschool program. Don't choose a school on the basis of its having a resident Apple or IBM or even a bank of them. If there is a computer in the school, check out how it's being used. Is it teaching purely academic skills by drill? Is there too much emphasis on which children can "do computer"? Or, rather, is it being used for short periods, with teacher supervision and with creative rather than drill programs (Springboard's *Mask Parade,* for example). If pressure for a computer in school comes up, raise some of the issues we've raised with the teacher, director, and other parents. Take a look at the available software programs before you buy a machine. Ask yourselves the tough question: "Is this the best use of preschool funds?"

The important thing a parent can do is to be a party to what a child is watching at home. Often when a preschooler is at home for some time before a parent comes home from work, someone—a sitter or a relative—may be choosing the channel. If a child is watching adult programs, echoes of those, too, can get into the classroom. *Rambo* or *Miami Vice* do not make for great preschool play. Young children acting out violent and/or adult video make trouble for teachers and for other children. As a partner to your child's preschool education, you can see to it that he or she does not watch the kind of programs that are harmful or that bring inappropriate concepts from TV or VCR into the preschool classroom.

In all forms of video, watch what your preschooler watches. Make sure it's appropriate. *Sesame Street, Mr. Rogers,* and *The Muppets* are all shows appropriate for young children. They will be enjoyable and will more likely be a social link with other kids. Watch with your child if possible. Notice how your child acts during and after a program or cassette. That may be your best clue as to whether he or she should be watching. Sometimes preschoolers get aggressive after watching certain shows. Many young children become frightened or weepy watching adult themes.

Limit the time spent in front of the TV set. It's tempting to use the tube as a baby-sitter, but an hour a day for a youngster of two to five is plenty. A recent survey by the University of Michigan's Social Research Institute says

Three children dress up to act out a fantasy train ride.

that the children of working mothers watch an average of 111 minutes a day, while nonworking mothers' youngsters watch 130 minutes per day! Better for children to spend the rest of the time outdoors or doing something where they power the action instead of the video character. The point is TV or VCR should not be cutting into time spent with either books or real-life experiences.

SPECIAL ISSUES

L et's take a look now at some of the special issues that may come up during the course of preschool. Actually, many of these "specials" aren't separate from the rest of a child's learning and growing. They could come up even if a child doesn't go to preschool. But how you as a parent feel about them and what you do about them has special meaning in terms of your child's life, in preschool and out.

TESTING

Sometime during your child's preschool years (possibly even before it begins) you may be told that the preschool wants to test your youngster. How should you feel about it?

Standardized tests of preschoolers may be given for a number of reasons. Sometimes the preschool program is part of a university study or an educational experiment. In that case the school needs to keep accurate records that measure how children are doing in a particular preschool program. Another reason for testing is that occasionally a school may suspect a physical or emotional problem that testing a youngster can help pinpoint. For example, Ben, the five-year-old of a neighbor, didn't seem to be listening or paying attention to what was going on around him. The teacher wasn't sure what his problem was, but she thought it might be his eyesight, so she talked with his parents about ordering a vision test for him. It turned out in this case that Ben had sudden-onset diabetes, a childhood form of diabetes that can cause eye problems.

Obviously these kinds of tests make sense. They're done with prior observation and knowledge of the young person and are designed to help the child or the program in some way. But there's another kind of testing that may not have such a sensible rationale behind it. Often independent schools will ask to have a four- or five-year-old tested as part of the admissions procedure. They may say that it is to establish a set of "base data" and to see if the child is developing according to "norms." The tests most frequently used by independent schools are the Stanford-Binet and the Wechsler Preschool and Primary Scales (WPPSI). Lucille Porter of Educational Records Bureau, which administers the tests for New York City independent schools, says that test results are only one factor in deciding whether a child is to be accepted into a school. An interview and evaluation from a previous preschool are the other factors that count. But our feeling is that if your child hasn't been to preschool before, then presumably the test score weighs more heavily. And in this kind of test, the chance for error abounds.

It's a familiar scene. A child is being tested for entry into preschool. The tester is asking questions. The child is restless, scared. The school explains to the parents that the test is part of its admissions procedure. But the child is uneasy, contrary that day. She may be thinking, "I'm going to zip up my mouth and not talk."

Children have usually never seen the tester before and may not perform well for a stranger. In addition, when children are given a standard intelligence test such as WPPSI, parents never get a chance to see the actual test results, although they pay for the test and for a conference in which the results are discussed. The most practical reason for resisting placement tests for a preschooler is that most tests do not measure things that it is important for a preschool to know about a child. And considering the fact that children grow and develop in fits and starts, one shouldn't put too much store in a test taken during one hour of a four-year-old's life. Some psychologists' research indicates that intelligence may have many facets and that IQ tests do not measure all of them. Lots of things may influence the score that a preschooler gets on so-called intelligence tests, not the least of which is being in a strange place and/or with a strange person.

Because many factors affect test scores (especially with young children), it is possible for a single test score to be a complete fluke. That fluke, however, could keep your child out of a certain school altogether or cast a child into a grouping that can follow him or her all through school. The worst of it is that both a parent and a child may come to accept the test results. In this sense it can be a self-fulfilling prophecy. Where a child tests exceptionally well, it may give a false or one-sided picture and may put undue pressure on a youngster to keep up an impossibly high standard of performance. Where a child has tested low, it can be damaging to self-esteem and even to how a parent feels about a youngster.

Here's one example of how unreliable standardized testing can be. Recently New York State began an experimental pre-K program open to parents of poor families. One of the Bank Street evaluators of the program, Anne Mitchell, had this to say: "Many parents wanted their children to be in the program because they wanted them to do well in school. In order to get in, the child must score *low* on the test. These parents, who very much wanted their children to succeed, were faced with a very strange situation: encouraging failure instead of success. They had to encourage their children to fail the test in order to get into the program that was going to help them succeed. In another site where low test scores were the admission ticket, parents reported coaching their children to fail because the parents were in desperate need of child care. Getting their child into the full-day pre-kindergarten program was their child care solution."

These are obviously pretty rare cases. But I know of their counterpart in a school for academically gifted children, where parents managed to get hold of copies of entrance tests and tutored their children. The anxiety that this kind of testing causes to both parents and children far outweighs any possible benefits in terms of information.

To sum up, preadmissions tests at this level are not by any means routine. But when they are given as an admissions requirement, they are often used to separate children and to label them. Youngsters may then wear these labels all through their school careers. For the ones with high scores, the label can be a source of pressure. For the lower scorers, Stanford-Binet and Wechsler can be a millstone around their necks.

Sue Bredenkamp, director of Early Childhood Programs for NAEYC, said in a recent article in *Principal* magazine, ''Standardized testing is not in the best interests of young children.'' And Jan Miller, director of City and Country School, which doesn't test its preschoolers, says that she finds it much more useful to evaluate children for admission by observing them for a whole day.

How Parents Can Help

As a general rule, if a school wants to test your preschooler, you should certainly find out why. If its purpose is only screening for placement, you may want to object.

Testing for placement occurs mainly in urban areas where there is a lot of competition for a relatively small number of places in a prestigious independent preschool. In this environment it's easy for a parent to get caught up in the idea of the desirability of his child going to the Ivy League of nursery schools. But there are several things to consider here. The most important one is that there are many excellent and highly thought-of preschools where testing is not part of the admissions procedure. The second thing to weigh is whether you want your child in a place where so much emphasis is put on standardized tests. Ask yourself whether the school's philosophy squares with yours in all other ways. If it does, then you'll have to decide whether it is worth it to subject your child to the kind of test that most early childhood educators think of as inappropriate.

There is little you can do about a school's admission procedures. It is not illegal to test youngsters in private schools, and you generally cannot get a school to make an exception if that is their way. If you feel really strongly about standardized testing of preschoolers for placement, your best move is to apply to a good preschool that doesn't do it.

What about standardized testing that comes up after a child has been going to preschool for a while? Here again, there are some specific differences parents should know about between testing in elementary school and preschool. In elementary school, teachers are much more accountable for teaching a given body of knowledge. Tests are given to all the children, but in a sense they are given to test the teacher as well as the students. In good preschools, on the other hand, there is a different set of expectations. Parents and teachers of preschoolers should not be looking to test the achievement or aptitudes that can be quantified on standard tests. It is not important here whether a child has an IQ of 120 or 140 or whether the child learned the alphabet. What is important is each child's total growth and development and the preschool's ability to foster it through appropriate activities.

If something seems to get in the way of this process, the teacher will usually pick up on it. Most schools will let you know if a child needs to be tested in any formal way. The teacher or director will share with you the purpose of the test and why she feels it is necessary. Often you'll have had a chance to talk about the problem with the teacher, and the testing of the child will be a joint decision. Sometimes she'll ask for a conference; sometimes you will. In this case you need to be thoroughly informed about the purpose of the test and the reason for it. If you still don't want the test administered, you can refuse, but the school can, if it feels strongly, refuse to keep your child. When in doubt, try to think about which stance will be better for your child.

To sum up—testing can be useful

▲ If a child is enrolled in an innovative school program (such as Head Start or Learning Through the
Arts), where records of individual learners can help
to evaluate all children

• In the event that a child has been in preschool a
while and the teacher suspects a physical or a learning
problem

But in both of these cases it is important for you and
the preschool to be in communication. Otherwise you'll be
worried, your child will sense your concern, and the test
may be skewed as a result.

Is there any preschool evaluating that makes sense? Yes.
Simple, informal records kept during a school year can
help teacher, parent, and child. After the first adjustment
weeks of school are over, a teacher may fill out a "profile"
sheet on a child based on her performance of certain basic
tasks and then fill one out again toward the end of the
year. Children's Underground Day Care Center, for example, looks at how children enjoy each activity, from
water play to books; at whether children are more often
alone than with other children; at whether they accept
routines and enjoy contributing to the group. These kinds
of observations help them to decide how a child is doing.

Keeping informal records of how each child performs is
good preschool practice, and parents should welcome it. It
means that the school thinks enough of your youngster to
record a set of "base data" to use to measure progress over
the year or years when your child will be in preschool.
Toward the end of the year the child is given the same
informal evaluation, and this is compared with what she
did at the beginning of the year. When this is put together
with what the teacher knows about the child and is pooled
with the parents' special insights about him or her, a

pretty good picture of the child's development can emerge. But it should be kept in mind that the real purpose of evaluations of young children is so that the partnership can make the most of preschool. It is not a test or a competition.

If a school doesn't keep a written evaluation sheet, it certainly doesn't mean a lack of interest. Many preschools keep a record of children's progress by other means, including careful observation.

A good preschool teacher is trained to observe everything about a child, from how he holds a pencil or crayon to what kind of block structures he builds. If there is a great gap between how well a youngster can talk and the kinds of things he can do, then the teacher will try to bring his *performance* into sync with his verbal skills. This kind of evaluation and diagnosis is a most useful form of testing.

Anne Mitchell says, ''Tests are designed to measure what is easiest to measure. In early childhood, that is basic cognitive functioning (and certain aspects of physical development). But the real success story of early childhood is played out in the social and emotional realm—fostering the disposition to learn and the motivation to succeed—for which there are no tests. Program evaluation procedures must be designed to reflect the complex nature of early childhood.''

DIVORCE, SEPARATION, SINGLES

Wendy, four years old, has been in preschool for several weeks. Her mother and father are separated. Her dad has custody, and Wendy has just about gotten used to this new arrangement. Now her mother decides that she wants custody of Wendy. A new agreement is drawn up that gives

Mom custody for part of each week—Tuesdays and Wednesdays.

Then one Friday her mother says to the preschool teacher, "I'd like to pick Wendy up today and take her with me for the weekend." The teacher says, "According to our schedule, your husband is supposed to pick her up today. If you're going to pick up instead, have him call us." A little while later, Dad calls and tells the school to tell Wendy that she will be going with her mother this weekend.

The preschool director said, "We told Wendy and she fell apart. She screamed and cried for two hours and yelled, 'I hate my mommy,' over and over again. It was predictable. We knew that Wendy would have a hard time with this shifting of plans. Children need and want consistency in their lives. A four-year-old can manage, with help, the idea of being with Mom part of the week and with Dad the other part. But you can't keep changing the rules and not expect a reaction."

Although in 1987 the breakup rate went down a bit, almost half of the marriages in the United States still wind up in divorce. Indeed, many more children are born these days without any marriage vows having been exchanged and, in many cases, without two parents in the picture. At the same time, another part of our culture is deeply rooted in traditional family values. It is sometimes hard for preschool teachers and for many parents to acknowledge fully the variety of arrangements under which the children of today live and under which they are being asked to cope with home and preschool.

HOW TEACHERS CAN HELP

Teachers, as part of the partnership, need to remember that a certain youngster has no dad at home or that another youngster's parents are in the midst of a separation. It's no fun for a child to be told, ''Take this note home to your mother'' if Mom isn't around. Teachers should also be alert for signals from a child that indicate problems at home and try to get to the root of them by contacting parents. If a teacher has a feeling there is something she doesn't know that is affecting a child's behavior, it is appropriate for her to ask, ''Anything going on at home that I should know about? Andrew has been upset lately.''

Parents should not resent this questioning for the child's benefit. On the other hand, teachers need to keep their distance from parental squabbling and from any appearance of favoring one parent over another in most disputes. A preschool's real role is to be an advocate for the child, not to take sides with either parent.

Young children often accept differences in life-styles better than grown-ups do. Whether a child has a stepfather or his mother a boyfriend are not conversational topics usually brought up by two-, three-, and four-year-olds. However, finding other kids in the same or similar situation can be one of the benefits of preschool, and a good teacher will see to it that some acknowledgment is made of differences in life-styles, without judgments being made.

How Parents Can Help

For parents, there are powerfully important reasons for communication between home and school about your particular family situation. If you've just been divorced or separated or newly remarried, or if you have a new partner, your child will probably be trying to understand and adjust. This may put him or her under some stress. Although you might not see it, the teacher may. The teacher and the school can help your child with the adjustment if they know where the stress is coming from. Children in recently divorced families may tend to be anxious or aggressive, dependent, disobedient, or whiny temporarily. Where parents and teachers work together, these characteristics gradually diminish.

Another good reason for giving the school the facts is for the protection of your youngster, especially in the case of split-ups that have turned nasty. You must protect the child. Always tell the school who is going to bring him and pick him up. If someone other than a parent will be picking him up, send a note. If a child is involved in custody litigation or if you suspect that the other parent or partner might try to get the child, tell the school immediately.

Remember that young children often don't fully understand war between parents. If a two- or three-year-old sees Daddy come to pick him up unexpectedly, he's not going to know that Daddy is trying to claim him so that he can whisk him out of state, nor is a school supposed to figure it out. No reliable teacher will release a child to a stranger, but if she knows it's Daddy and if the child seems happy, she can be forgiven for assuming that everything is okay unless she has been told otherwise.

A LAST WORD

In any kind of marital or other relationship problem, both parents and teachers have a responsibility to the child. Children are powerless, and they can be hurt. Parents need to explain divorce, separation, and other family changes in terms that a child can understand. Youngsters need help in adjusting to new "significant others" in their parents' lives and in their own.

If you're at a loss as to how to explain family matters of this kind to your child, the preschool may be able to give you guidance. Sometimes reading a book to a child helps. Some of the books on the subject that we recommend are

Mom and Dad Don't Live Together Anymore, by Kathy Stinson (Annick Press, Toronto); *Mommy and Daddy Are Fighting,* by Susan Paris (The Seal Press); *Jennifer Has Two Daddies,* by Priscilla Galloway (The Women's Educational Press); and *Two Homes to Live In,* by Barbara Shook Hazen (Human Sciences Press).

The teacher can help you with your child, but parents should not involve teacher or the preschool director in the nuts and bolts of family problems, such as asking for advice on alimony, names of lawyers, or other matters that are not the school's province. If you're at a loss about what to do in a marital crisis, you should consider counseling. A teacher can help the child express her feelings, but she can't take sides. And she's not a therapist—neither yours nor your child's.

THE HANDICAPPED PRESCHOOLER

Joshua has cerebral palsy. Kim is a slow learner. David has severe vision problems. Althea is unable to form words. Marco is so extremely antisocial that he can't be with other children.

All of these preschoolers are handicapped children who have special needs. The Council for Exceptional Children defines "special needs" children as children who differ significantly from other children their age. All children grow at their own rate, and some reach certain stages before or after their peers, but in some cases a child's emotional or physical development is so different that he needs special help in achieving his full potential.

It is important to give children such as Joshua, Kim, and others help as early as possible—at three or even earlier. There is a trend lately toward "mainstreaming"— that is, putting handicapped youngsters in preschool classrooms with children who are not handicapped. The idea behind it is that both handicapped and nonhandicapped children have to be prepared to live in the real world and to learn to appreciate, accept, and understand one another. Having a handicapped child in preschool has some special ramifications for the child, his parents, the teacher, and the other parents and children in the center.

IF YOUR CHILD IS HANDICAPPED

Placing a handicapped young child in a mainstream setting is a big decision—both for the parents and for the preschool. Following are some of the factors that a parent needs to take a look at.

One of the things that you have to consider is the nature of your child's handicap. You know your own child better than the preschool does, and even though it is going to have to be a shared decision, you have to be honest enough to look at your own child and decide whether mainstreaming is sensible for him. I saw a child with cerebral palsy doing well in a child care center (see page 95), but this particular child wasn't severely handicapped. He couldn't walk unaided, but his speech and small-motor coordination were good enough for him to be able to work with some manipulative toys and to participate in other group activities.

If you make your decision to look in the mainstream for a preschool for your youngster, you can approach the search just as any other parent would. Keep in mind that many of your child's basic needs are the same as those of other children. When you've decided on a specific preschool and the preschool has agreed to accept your youngster, spend some time there and imagine your child in the setting with those teachers. Then, when you and your child visit, watch how the teachers act with your child. Do they seem uncomfortable with his handicap? Are they overly solicitous? Study how they are with other children. Do they seem alert to each child as an individual? Your child will have a better chance of being comfortable where the setting already supports differences—whether it is in dress, behavioral style, or skin color.

PARENTS AND HANDICAPPED CHILDREN

There's probably no place where it's more important for parents and teachers to work together as a team than where a handicapped child is being mainstreamed. A parent needs to tell a teacher everything that could be useful to her in integrating a handicapped child into a preschool program. Using the examples of handicapped children mentioned at the beginning of the section: Four-year-old David is almost blind and he's afraid of loud noises. Knowing this, his teacher in preschool can ease him into tolerating music time by taking him out of the room at first, then later warning him when the "marching band" is going to start and staying with him. Three-year-old Althea, who has been identified as having learning deficits, is apt to have a temper tantrum when she can't do something or can't get what she wants. It may be slightly embarrassing for Althea's mother and dad to reveal this about Althea before she starts school, but it will be of immeasurable help to the teacher in giving this particular three-year-old a good preschool experience.

It is doubly important for a parent of a handicapped child to stay in touch with the child's preschool and to visit often. For one thing, you can use the support you'll get from the teacher and the director. For another, you can learn some things from seeing normal children in action that will give you new insights into your own child. You may find that certain behavior you thought was a result of your child's handicap is common to the age group. You'll get a new view of what your child is capable of and you'll have a chance to enjoy the confirmation that your youngster can function as part of a group in spite of some limitations.

TEACHERS AND HANDICAPPED CHILDREN

Teachers have an enormously important role to play in the success of the handicapped child in a mainstream preschool. A good teacher will learn all she can about the specific handicap of the child in her group. She'll arrange to spend some time alone with the child before he joins the group so that she can get to know him. She'll prepare the other children for his coming by casually telling two or three children at a time that a handicapped child will be joining the group and asking them to help make him feel comfortable. She won't make too much of it. She'll phase him in slowly, getting a feel for what he can and can't do and being careful not to overprotect him while making sure that she's not asking too much of him.

One of the things that a good preschool teacher thinks about is the other children in the group and what having a handicapped child may mean to each of them. Sometimes a sensitive youngster will react very personally to a child's handicap and worry that it will happen to her. A withered arm may be frightening to some children; stuttering may make some children laugh. The teacher tries to find out what the children are feeling and deal with it without making either the handicapped or the normal child feel guilty.

WHEN MAINSTREAMING IS NOT POSSIBLE

If your child is autistic, like Marco (above) turned out to be, or if he's violently disruptive, it's better for him to be in a setting where he can't hurt other children and where he gets specific help by trained professionals. Jean Pole-shuck, a specialist who works with autistic children in the Newark, New Jersey, public schools, feels that certain learning delays and neurological problems are helped more by starting early in a setting geared to the handicapping condition. She points out that because so much learning takes place at the preschool ages, it's important for some handicapped children to get professional help at that time. It may be better for your handicapped child to get specific help now in preschool and join the mainstream later. This is a decision that you and a professional (doctor or psychologist) should make together. But one thing that may make your decision easier is the realization that special education at the preschool level can often maximize your child's potential for going to school in the mainstream later.

There are special programs available for preschoolers both in and out of mainstream settings. As I mentioned earlier, Head Start is required by law to enroll 10 percent handicapped children regardless of income. In addition, in 1986 federal legislation was enacted to expand the federal mandate for the education of handicapped children to include children from birth to five years old. This legislation, often referred to as Part B, focuses on children three to five. Twenty-one states, Puerto Rico, and the Virgin Islands already have programs designed to serve handicapped preschoolers. Florida expects things to be in place by early 1989. So does Nevada. Fifteen additional states have mandates for such programs by 1990.

ONE FINAL NOTE

If your child is normal and she's in a preschool classroom with a handicapped child, both you and she may have some feelings about it. You may wonder whether it is good for your child to be in a class with, for example, a child who is slightly brain damaged and has a speech impediment that your child is beginning to mimic. Or you may feel that the teacher is taking too much time away from the other children to cater to the special needs of the handicapped child. These feelings are shared by many parents and are worth talking over with the teacher or director of your preschool.

If your child seems distressed or frightened by a handicapped child, try to get him to talk about his fears. Then you can help him deal with them. It will be one more aspect of his preschool learning.

EMOTIONAL PROBLEMS

It is hard to imagine anyone's life being completely free of depression, anxiety, or stress. Take stress, for example. Children, like adults, face stress at certain times. There is no way that human beings can entirely avoid it, and as a matter of fact, there is good solid evidence that a certain amount of stress can be a useful catalyst and energizer. Children who learn to cope with stress and to understand its messages in relation to their own bodies and personalities generally gain confidence and have good feelings about themselves.

However, occasionally a child begins to behave in a way that seems to say that he or she is not functioning well, either as a result of too much stress or for some other reason.

Sometimes the teacher will notice: "Beryl is always complaining of a stomachache lately." "Johann sits in the corner by himself far too much."

Sometimes it's a parent who becomes concerned: "Tommy isn't eating and seems so listless." "Meg is waking up with nightmares every night."

More often, if preschool and parents are working together, it's a joint discovery : The teacher may say, "Adam seems extremely nervous. He has developed a stutter and blinks his eyes constantly."

The parent says, "Yes, I'm concerned. He's doing the same thing at home."

It's important to know that any one of these symptoms could show up in a child and not be cause for alarm. Children go through the stages of growing up in different ways. Some perfectly normal youngsters have nightmares, stutter, develop a tic, appear nervous, have stomach upsets, experience headaches, overeat, undereat, or get depressed or anxious at certain times. Such symptoms often pass.

So, the appearance of even a few of these symptoms is not necessarily a cause for immediate concern. The important factor is how long the behavior persists. If it continues, something needs to be done. Psychologist Leah Levinger cautions that there is an exception to this general "take it slow" rule. Some behavior needs immediate attention—sudden screaming or nightmares that surface for no apparent reason, or if your youngster suddenly starts pulling out his hair or biting himself and drawing blood. These are real cries for help and have to be answered immediately.

It is usually hard for a parent to accept the idea that a child may have a problem. But if you find yourself in that situation, try not to be too angry or resentful. No reputable school wants to make problems for a parent. If teachers tell you something about your child, you can feel pretty sure that they have thought about it and had a number of consultations with other teachers before alerting you. Look on it as a benefit that the school may have discovered something that can be remedied. Don't try to sweep the problem under the rug, as this parent did :

Three-year-old Daniel's mother had noticed that he

wasn't as coordinated as other boys his age. But she told herself that it was because he was upset over her recent divorce. (Many parents blame divorce for their children's problems, not always accurately.) She convinced herself that he didn't talk because he had a non-English-speaking sitter. She had read a book about parenting that said, "Don't compare." So she tried not to.

But at preschool the teachers noticed pretty quickly that Daniel's muscle tone was poor and that his language development was not what it should be at three years of age. They waited a few months. His language picked up a bit, but his coordination didn't improve. After three or four months the school was convinced that Daniel had more than a passing problem. The school suggested that a social worker take a look at Daniel, and she confirmed that Daniel had some combination of physical and emotional problems that needed further looking into. Here is what followed in this particular instance:

First the teacher met with Dan's mother in an effort to persuade her to follow up on Dan's problem. But in this case Dan's mother said, "Daniel is perfectly normal," and refused to take any further steps.

The school was concerned for Dan's future if he remained without help. They began to insist. Dan's mother became angry and blamed the school for Dan's problem. Her attitude seemed to be, "If you hadn't stirred this up, we would have all been better off." She removed Daniel from the school rather than face the truth of his handicap. Later the school discovered that Daniel had been enrolled for a relatively short while in another preschool program before he had come to them. His mom was doing what preschool directors refer to as "center hopping" in order to avoid dealing with his problem.

There are a fair number of preschoolers who are in the

same boat as Daniel. However, they don't have to wind up
as Daniel did, squeezed between a parent who denies the
problem and a preschool that may not have tried hard
enough to win the parent's cooperation.

How Parents Should Help

What do you do if you and/or the preschool feel the time
has come to act? Child psychologists usually recommend
that parents turn first to their pediatrician or family doctor. There are many behavioral symptoms that have physical causes. Inattention and poor speech can indicate a
hearing problem. Hyperactivity can be caused by diet.
Depression and bed-wetting can have a physical cause. It's
worth it to go this route first. And there's good reason to
go to a doctor who knows the child, because she has records
and can best evaluate the changes that you've noticed.

Should everything check out on the physical side, the
view of many child psychologists is still conservative as
far as treatment is concerned. A number of them feel that
the next step for a parent would be to take a look at what
may be going on at home. If, for instance, a beloved
grandma has just died, then a child's depression can perhaps be better understood and dealt with.

Not all emotional problems are this clear-cut, however.
In cases where parents can't figure out the answers, often
the preschool can help. And occasionally, it works the other
way. It's always possible that some situation in preschool
has triggered a child's change in behavior. Here is another
place where rapport and partnership between preschool
and home can work for the benefit of your child.

In some preschools psychological consultation is available. Sometimes this service is free (for instance, in Head
Start and in some pre-K programs), sometimes it's ar-

ranged by the preschool, sometimes the preschool has a referral person or source. This person may advise certain tests to help diagnose your child's problem. You should know that there are specific tests that can help pinpoint certain neurological/learning disorders or emotional problems, and these tests can be important.

If your preschool doesn't offer this kind of help, you'll want to turn to community agencies. My own community has a Bureau of Children's Services for each of several sparsely populated counties. In trying to get in touch with them as a concerned parent would, I discovered more than a little red tape. That's precisely what you do not need when you are worried. So my sense would be to try to get the preschool or child care center to help you find help.

There is some evidence that long hours in day care and the strain of separation from parents may account for increasing symptoms of stress in some young children. There is also evidence that the drive toward early mastery of academic skills is triggering anxiety and other signs of stress in some children. Some stress may be due to the increasingly stressful lives that today's adults lead. Emotional problems, say some psychologists, can be "passed on," something like contagious diseases, from parents to children.

Perhaps the most constructive thing a parent can do for a child is to try to control undue stress and tension. Some things, such as separation and divorce, moving, a death in the family, can't be helped. And the fact is that children are pretty tough. Most of them can cope with changes in their lives pretty successfully in the long run. Some of them even cope well with a fair amount of pressure and stress. However, if you're a Type A personality and your child does *not* seem to be thriving emotionally, or if the school suggests that you may be expecting too much of your young citizen, you will want to look at what goes on in your family.

What form will the help take? Sometimes it may just be a single consultation with a psychologist that will help define the problem and suggest a course of action. Other times a psychologist may suggest that the whole family work together with him on the problem. Occasionally a professional will suggest therapy for the child.

WHEN YOU AND THE PRESCHOOL DISAGREE

What happens if something comes up and you and the teacher simply don't see eye-to-eye? If you've both tried and it is not getting resolved, then you may have to make an appeal to the next level of responsibility—in most cases, the director of the preschool. Sometimes the director will agree with you, sometimes with the teacher. Many times, if she's experienced, she'll work out a compromise that satisfies both of you and preserves your relationship with each other and with the child.

But what about a severe disagreement where you think the school is dead wrong? It may be good to pause here for a minute and look at the complete chain of appeal in a preschool confrontation.

There's a good reason why your first step should normally be the teacher. If you start by going over the teacher's head, the partnership you're working so hard to forge will surely be affected. So, unless the issue is one you just can't talk to her about, go to your child's teacher first. If this doesn't work, then your next appeal, as I've said, is to the director.

If you are still unsatisfied, you have a few options. If your preschool is a not-for-profit center, there is a board of directors and you can appeal to it. Here is a case in point : Several parents at a child care center were convinced that the conduct of one of the teachers was unprofessional and negligent. Although they talked with the teacher individually and collectively, they got nowhere. The director supported the teacher. The parents felt that in this case her loyalty was misplaced. So they went to the board of trustees of the school and presented their evidence. Shortly thereafter the teacher was dismissed.

What happens if you don't have a board of trustees to appeal to ? In some settings there is a private owner of the preschool to whom you have recourse, and this is always a possibility. For certain issues there may be a local government agency whose help you can enlist. For example, one parent decided that the food served in a child's preschool (bread and potato salad as a lunch menu !) was downright unhealthy. The preschool director refused to change or modify the menus. The parents finally appealed to the local Board of Children and Youth Services, which oversees health standards and licensing procedures in their community. The Board forced the school to adhere to dietary standards. But by this time the parents' confidence in the school had become eroded, and they took their child out of the school.

In another case the issue that came to a confrontation was raised by the teacher rather than the parent. The teacher came to the parent suggesting that the child might need help for an emotional disturbance. She suggested a conference with a local social agency. The parent said there was nothing wrong with the child and refused to get a professional opinion. The preschool, which felt that the other children were being affected by the child's disruptive behavior, did not take him back the following semester.

243

In both of these cases it should be noted that the child was taken out of preschool. And that is, of course, the final recourse—child and preschool part company. Sometimes it's the best way—indeed, the only way. That is, incidentally, one of the big differences between preschool and later elementary school. You can take your child out of preschool; in public elementary school it is much harder to do. In any case, before you pull your child out, you should first do everything possible to keep the situation from coming to that.

A FINAL WORD

Here are a few points to keep in mind regarding disagreements:

▲ One good way to avoid confrontational issues is to check the preschool out thoroughly before your child starts (see chapter 3). Make sure you fully understand the school's policies on everything from discipline to hiring and firing teachers.

• If an issue arises, be willing to listen and soberly consider the teacher's point of view, even if it's not what you want to hear or you don't agree with it.

▪ Allow time for the director and/or other officials to study an issue you raise. Don't expect an administrator to act on your complaint without an investigation.

▲ Whatever happens, try not to let your disagreement with a particular preschool color your youngster's feelings about all preschools. There is no need to share all the details of the brouhaha with your four-year-old. In fact, as in a divorce, it's better for the child to remain on good terms with the partner (in this case the preschool) than to erode her confidence in teachers and child care settings altogether.

MULTICULTURAL FAMILIES AND PRESCHOOL

A family's background and culture inevitably contribute to how that family looks at preschool. For some families, like those newly arrived here from other countries, there are language and cultural differences that may make it difficult to find a good program fit. For others there may be financial problems. And for still others it is the worry

A preschool with a multicultural character benefits all its youngsters.

that preschool will not serve the needs of their child, educationally or culturally, because some of their interests and their contributions are not reflected in the programs.

According to the National Black Child Development Institute, many black parents have special concerns about preschool and their children. Nancy Bryant, a spokesperson of NBCDI, says, "Black parents are scared that their kids need something—that if they don't get started in school early, the kids will lag behind."

This perhaps explains why in one urban preschool a black parent told the director that she thought her child needed a more structured environment than the school was providing. She said, ''We both know that my child isn't going to get as good an education as a white middle-class child. I need for her to get started early in academics. I want her to learn her numbers and letters so that she'll have a chance of keeping up.''

Many parents share this view that their children need a more structured academic beginning to equip them for later schooling. But minority parents especially seem to feel that their youngsters cannot afford the luxury of ''learning to learn'' at their own pace. It's hard to argue with the fact that a Hispanic, Asian, or black youngster from a poor family is generally going to go into the system under a handicap. We know for a fact that poor school districts get fewer good teachers and less funding, when it should be just the other way around. However, there is no proof that worksheets and drill in preschool are the answers to the problem. The proof seems to flow in the other direction; the preschool programs that seem to offer the best start for any youngster are the ones that focus on children's overall development.

Studies that have followed children from both academic and developmental preschool programs through later schooling give evidence that children gain in significant ways from developmental programs. Children who attended developmental rather than academic programs had a lower dropout rate as well as a lower incidence of delinquency. The abilities that set the stage for later school and personal success appear to be a taste for learning, a sense of one's self, and an ability to get along with other people. In early childhood it seems to be at least as important for a child to learn self-esteem and independence; how to focus attention; how to listen to a story; how to share ideas, follow instructions, and learn to cooperate in a group as it is to learn letters and numbers.

Why is it that a developmental program can do these things while a more formal program cannot? The reason that a developmental program works is that it takes into consideration all kinds of children. Because it looks at individuals, it can give each child what he needs. The result is that all kinds of bias, including cultural bias, disappear. Each child is free to learn and grow according to his innate ability—and to develop a great sense of himself.

RACIAL ISSUES IN SCHOOL

Darlene and Chris are playing at the water table in a child care center. There are both a white and a brown doll in the water.

Darlene says, "I'm going to play with that baby." (She points to the white doll.)

Chris says, "You can't. You have to play with the brown baby because you're a brown girl." (He snatches the white doll from Darlene.)

Darlene is sad. "But I want to play with the white baby," she says.

There's nothing new about a black child preferring a white doll. In the early 1940s psychologists Kenneth Clark and Mamie Clark tested a number of black children and discovered that two-thirds of the black children preferred white dolls, considering the black dolls less beautiful and less intelligent. Forty years later Dr. Clark repeated his experiment and discovered that about the same proportion of black children went for the white dolls. In other words, it is possible that as many black children today feel a sense of racial inferiority as did children of forty years ago, though whether the intensity of that feeling has changed is another matter.

Even the best preschool cannot solve deeply entrenched problems of racial inequality, but it can do its part on the educational level. Feelings of inferiority of any sort are not good feelings for children to have. So a good preschool offers brown dolls and fosters respect for the people who share their color. A wise parent of any race supports the effort and talks directly about it even with a three-year-old.

Another vivid example of the way children's minds work is a story we heard from a teacher in a child care center that prides itself on its multicultural character. A black mother came to school upset because her child had come home saying he wanted to be white. The mother thought that surely discrimination must be behind his desire to give up his racial pride. But it turned out that that was not the case. His best friend, who admired his chocolate skin, had told him he wished he were black; the black child had simply returned the compliment.

Racial and ethnic issues do come up in preschool. Young children are not color blind. They ask questions that deserve thoughtful answers. In a good preschool, trained teachers know how to handle the questions and statements that come out of the mouths of babes. Parents of all races and ethnic backgrounds can help support what the school is trying to do.

Child Abuse

Like all formerly taboo subjects, the abuse of young children is coming under new scrutiny. In the face of evidence that a few of the cases of child abuse may have taken place in school, parents can't help but feel that here's yet another issue to deal with and worry about while their child is in someone else's care.

There is no question that sexual abuse of children is widespread. Whether it is more or less prevalent or simply more widely reported than it used to be doesn't matter. What is clear is that most sexual abuse of children occurs within the family or with people who are not strangers. "Not in *my* house," we all say. But somehow having one's own house in order doesn't really feel like enough to protect a child. What should a parent do, or not do, to prevent sexual abuse to a child? How much should you tell a three-to-five-year-old?

At Bank Street we recently saw a video that was supposed to teach children how to protect themselves against abuse from strangers. In the film preschoolers were "trained" not to get too close to someone they didn't know and were shown how to back away from any person approaching them. They were instructed as to who was a friend ("someone you know") and who was to be avoided ("anyone you don't know through your parents"). I was uncomfortable watching the tape, as were my Bank Street colleagues. It was too simple; it had too many possibilities for misunderstanding. How could a young child ever get to know and trust a decent, caring adult under those rules? And where is the protection against a relative or someone you *do* know who is a potential abuser?

Psychologist Leah Levinger has concerns about giving young children a battery of explicit rules. Dr. Levinger maintains that a three-, four-, or five-year-old is both suggestible and unreliable. If you make too many rules and prescriptions about sensitive issues, such as unwanted touching, you run the risk of having a child misunderstand your message. Touching and cuddling have always been an important part of nursery and preschool programs. Should we expect kids to reject hugs, or to report them?

Here's another possibility for misunderstanding: A youngster goes to preschool, has diarrhea, and soils his pants. The teacher, in cleaning him up, touches his penis. The child, who has been warned about allowing anyone to touch him and who is uncomfortable during the cleanup to begin with, reports to his parents that the teacher touched him on his private parts. Being the carrier of such a tale puts an unfair burden on a child and can put a teacher or even a whole school in jeopardy—unjustly.

HOW PARENTS CAN HELP

Dr. Levinger feels that teaching about abuse to young children is the parents' job, not the school's. She recommends, first of all, that a parent lay down a few clear rules as early as possible about going anywhere with strangers. Says she, "It's like teaching a child not to run into the street." Beyond this, Levinger suggests that parents encourage youngsters in a general way to talk about everything that goes on in school and at home. If the lines of communication between child and parent are open, a child will be more apt to talk about any unusual behavior on the part of a teacher or aide, uncle or baby-sitter, even if she hasn't been told that a particular behavior is forbidden. Parents need to listen intelligently to what their children tell them and to be in close enough contact with the school so that they know what's going on there. It is unlikely that a preschool with a good reputation that welcomes visits by parents and keeps in close touch with them will have an abuse problem. Choosing a quality setting for your child is probably the best way of dealing with this ugly issue.

AIDS

AIDS is a fatal disease for which at this time there is no cure. It is caused by a virus known as HIV, and is transmitted by sexual contact or contact with infected blood or blood products. Of all the cases of AIDS so far reported, about 2 percent have been children. Most child AIDS victims get HIV from their mothers during pregnancy. A child infected with HIV can, under some circumstances, transmit it, but no case of AIDS has ever been transmitted in a child care setting. Still, every parent has questions about AIDS and preschoolers, because young children in preschool settings handle and mouth toys, touch each other, and share clothing. As AIDS continues to spread in the general population, it is conceivable that a child infected with AIDS or the HIV virus could be in your child's preschool. If so, what are the implications for your child and the child with HIV?

Dr. Susan Aronson, clinical professor of pediatrics at Hahnemann Hospital, Philadelphia, has studied AIDS risks for children in child care settings. She emphasizes the fact that the disease can't be spread by contact with urine, stool, vomit, tears, or saliva. Playing with an infected child's toys won't do it, nor will wiping a nose, hugging, playing with the same toy, or the usual things children do together in preschool.

What about biting? Aronson points out that an infected child would have to be a biter *and* be bleeding from a sore in the mouth at the time he or she bit in order to have any risk occur for the child who was bitten. That is, she says, "an unlikely event." If a healthy child were to bite an AIDS-infected child and draw blood, then the *biter* might be at risk.

The American Academy of Pediatrics emphasizes, in an

article in their November 1988 journal *Pediatrics,* that HIV is *not* highly contagious and that transmission requires repeated sexual contact or intravenous inoculation. It recommends that HIV be looked at as one of a number of blood-communicated diseases and suggests that all child care centers in areas where there is a high prevalence of the disease have in place the kinds of sanitary precautions that we outlined in the ''Health'' section of chapter 7. However, it emphasizes that these are maximum precautions, designed mainly to prevent contact with blood, and that even that contact on a one-time basis would pose little risk.

The Academy says that HIV-infected children should be admitted freely to all activities in child care centers, since most of them pose no risk to others. These children should be under ongoing medical evaluation, and if there are any questions about the safety of having a child in a day care or preschool setting, professionals with special expertise in AIDS and HIV infection should be available for consultation.

Should preschools and child care centers screen children for the presence of HIV? The doctors of the Academy say no. They point out that not only is the transmission of this disease in the child care setting totally hypothetical, the risk of getting a false-positive result in screening for it is quite high and will give many parents a great deal of unnecessary anxiety.

The panel of pediatricians recommends that no disclosure of a child's HIV status be given to other parents in a school setting, but that appropriate information about the child's status be given to caregivers to protect the child from other infections. They stress, however, that this information does not necessarily have to require knowledge of the child's HIV status.

HOW PARENTS CAN HELP

There are two sides to the AIDS discussion. One is the parent of the well child, the preschooler who is going to school and needs to be protected. Parents need to see to it that the preschool their child goes to has rigorous sanitation procedures in effect, especially with regard to first aid for cuts and any other occurrence where there is blood. This is obviously more important if you live in a place where there is a high incidence of AIDS.

The other side of the coin is the physical and mental health of the child who has HIV and is in preschool. Children who have contracted the AIDS virus through tainted blood—hemophiliacs, for instance—have been subjected to the double cruelty of having a serious health problem and being discriminated against. The children are too young to understand what's wrong with them, and they're often regarded as pariahs. Where such a child is in preschool and is known, all parents and caregivers owe it to him to be as caring as possible.

HIV-infected children are vulnerable to infections of all kinds. Certain childhood diseases could be fatal for them. Their special health needs are going to have to be addressed, and the parents of these youngsters need to make sure they are in settings where they have the facilities for this kind of special watching.

SAYING GOOD-BYE TO PRESCHOOL

I t's spring. Susan and Sam have been going to the same preschool for a couple of years now. Both children are five and are slated to start kindergarten in the fall. Both of them have gotten a lot out of their preschool experience, yet each of them has taken from it different things. For instance, Susan has learned a good bit about herself and other people. Sam has enjoyed a new competence in physical activities. Their teachers feel that both of them have much greater understanding of colors and shapes, numbers and letters, games and daily routines than they had when they came in. And Sam now has a much longer attention span than he had when he started preschool at three. Susan has shed some of her shyness and seems to look forward to new situations with little or no separation anxiety. Would all this have happened anyway? It's hard to say. In Susan's case her dad is convinced that preschool made a positive difference in her development.

Now these two pleasurable preschoolers are ready for kindergarten. It's time to get into the elementary school loop. But isn't kindergarten basically like preschool? And for that reason, can't you expect that your youngster will sail in, armed with her past experience? Yes and no. Regardless of the fact that your child has been to preschool, there are some things about most public school kindergartens that are significantly different from nursery school and other forms of preschool child care. Here are some recent impressions of parents we spoke to:

"Kindergarten today is harder—like first grade used to be when my oldest child was in school."

"Teachers there can't look at individual children the way the preschool teachers did. There are thirty kids in my child's class."

"They give tests now to see if your child is ready for kindergarten."

"My youngster didn't feel any pressure in his preschool, but he feels it in kindergarten."

All of these comments reflect some of the differences between preschool and many public and private kindergarten programs. Let's take a quick look at what happens when your child "graduates" from preschool to kindergarten and some of the things you as a parent can do to preserve a good preschool experience at the next level of education. (For a full and detailed look at kindergarten and beyond, see *The Elementary School Handbook* by Joanne Oppenheim, published by Pantheon.)

WHAT PARENTS SHOULD KNOW ABOUT KINDERGARTEN

In most states children are eligible for public kindergarten the year they are five if the fifth birthday occurs before October 1. But this doesn't mean they have to go. Kindergarten is not mandatory in most states, which is why a parent and/or a school district can decide that a child is not ready for kindergarten, that a child needs a special kind of kindergarten, or that a child can skip kindergarten altogether (though this is usually not a good idea). The kindergarten decision needs to be made carefully by you and the school together and should be based on as much information as possible. Here are a few things that you may want to think about in making such a decision:

▲ The closer children are to six years of age, the better they seem to do in public kindergarten.

• Generally speaking, girls who are on the young side do better than boys of the same age.

■ Independence and social skills as well as concrete hands-on experiences learned in preschool count for a great deal in kindergarten adjustment.

▲ Even if your youngster has preschool behind him, he may still not be ready for full-day kindergarten. If he has spent all day in a good developmental preschool, he could still find kindergarten wearing.

Kindergarten programs vary from school district to school district. Some few public kindergarten programs have a developmental outlook similar to our favored Type C preschool. But more of them are traditional and teacher-directed. This doesn't mean that a child who has come from a great Type C pre-K will necessarily flounder in a Type B kindergarten. What it could mean is a little confusion in the switch from "learning by doing" to "learning by ditto sheet." If you understand what's happening, you can help and support him. You may also find that you'll want to open up for discussion in your PTA the possibility of a more individualized approach to kindergarten.

WHEN A PARENT GOES TO KINDERGARTEN

Start looking ahead to kindergarten well before the time your child will be attending. One of the first things you should decide is which public (or private) school your child will be attending. Find out if you have any choices within the district, as parents have in certain cities, such as Minneapolis, Minnesota. Sometimes one kindergarten program is clearly better than another, but you can only know this if you do a little research. Keep in mind that although you may enroll your child for school during the summer, you won't be able to see the program in session unless you enroll him or her in the spring.

Often a public school will contact you before your child is enrolled. Sometimes the kindergarten teacher will come to visit. Sometimes there will be a little get-together of parents and children at the school. If you don't see any of this action shaping up in your neighborhood, call the school your child will be attending and ask when they are having an "open house" for new parents. This little call will serve a few purposes. If they are planning such an event, you'll be able to put it on your calendar. If they're not, your call will make it clear that you think it is appropriate for parents to visit and that you expect it. Indeed, you are entitled to it. It is also tremendously important to your child. How a youngster is welcomed into kindergarten can set the tone for the whole year, so be sure to make time for this socializing.

In one school I visited, the kindergarten teacher (a man, which was a pleasant surprise) always makes a welcome day for the upcoming kindergartners and their parents late in the spring. The veteran kindergartners act as hosts and make decorations for the walls that include the new children's names. There's a time for fun and games as well as a time for parents and teacher to get a chance to talk.

PRIVATE SCHOOL

Of course, public kindergarten is not your only option. You may decide that the local public school is poor or that your child was so happy in preschool that you want him to go to kindergarten (or whatever the school calls it) at the same private school. Similarly, you may want your youngster to have a parochial-school education or to be educated by the Quakers or in a Montessori or a Rudolf Steiner school. In some cities you can find almost any kind of private school you're seeking if you have the means. Even if you don't, there are schools that offer help.

The private-school-versus-public-school decision is similar to the one you had to make when you chose a preschool for your youngster. Many parents make the decision based on the quality of the neighborhood school. That's why you need to really check out what's going on there. One caution: It is usually not a good idea to make a judgment about the school based on hearsay from a parent. One parent's personal experience does not necessarily mean that a public school is not doing a good job. You need to go and take a look for yourself. You can usually tell pretty quickly what the educational climate is. For example, one parent whose youngster had thrived in a developmental preschool was told by the public school, ''The first thing we'll have to do is break his spirit.'' Fortunately this is a worst-case scenario. But the fact that it happens at all means that you may have to have a fall-back position.

HOW THE PRESCHOOL CAN HELP

The director of your son's or daughter's preschool is often the key to kindergarten information. Sometimes the school has a parent meeting devoted to talk about kindergarten and local options. Some preschools are in direct contact with each school their "graduates" will be attending. The Mekeel Center in East Stroudsburg, Pennsylvania, has a conference with the public school about each of its pre-schoolers who will be feeding into the school system. The public school can get valuable information this way, information that will help kindergarten teachers do the best job with your child.

Preschools also may provide the setting for the screening procedures that some public schools ask for. These tests are then sent to the schools to which the parents have applied. There is a growing tendency among public schools to administer readiness or maturity tests to help decide whether a child is ready for kindergarten or which kindergarten she may be ready for. One of the tests widely used by public schools is the Gesell School Readiness Test, which looks at many of the developmental signposts that a good preschool has been evaluating during the time your child has been there. (A private school may use other tests as their criteria, or may use no test, depending on the school.)

Test results certainly can be faulted (see "Testing," in chapter 9). The Gesell depends on a trained person to administer and interpret, and some research indicates that a child has a fifty-fifty chance of being misdiagnosed as un-ready by Gesell. But still, a parent should attempt to understand why the school is giving the test before resisting it. In general a school tests a youngster at the beginning of his school life to try to get a better picture of what he can do and how he can be placed in the most appropriate setting for him. For example, some schools now have ''developmental'' kindergartens, which are closer in feeling to a Model C preschool and are, in the opinion of some educators, more suitable than traditional kindergartens for younger and/or less mature entrants. If you are told that your child is going into a developmental kindergarten, don't regard it as your child's failure. It may prove to be the best thing that could happen to her. Developmental kindergartens are usually not plagued by the pressure-cooker atmosphere that seems so much a part of many of today's regular kindergartens. The ones we've seen felt like the children were learning with pleasure and that the teachers were looking at children's individual learning styles and were trying to make the most of them. In one school district they are talking of making all the kindergarten classes into developmental centers. This would free both teachers and children to set up learning priorities that are based on what a child is ready for. This may be a sound idea and a better transition from preschool.

We still think an informed portrait of a child by the preschool teacher and the other adults who know her best is a much sounder evaluation of her abilities than a single test. But a public school that is willing to augment test results by working with both parent and preschool is a good omen for parents who value the parent-school partnership. One thing parents should be wary of is the school system that advises, on the basis of a single test, that they keep a child out of kindergarten altogether because she's not ''ready.'' More often it is a school's lack of readiness to accommodate itself to an individual child that drives this kind of decision.

HELPING CHILDREN TO SAY GOOD-BYE

Early childhood consultant Alison Pepper points out that in a child's short life, preschool may have occupied the largest block of time. To ask a youngster to put all that behind her when she goes to kindergarten is to ask her to wipe out her own history. Pepper recommends that parents bring their children back to preschool for visits, both before kindergarten starts and after the child has been there for a while.

The former director of the Children's Underground says, "These visits accomplish two things. First, they remind the child of what she did and learned in this place. I was terrific when I was here, she remembers. I can be terrific in my new school. A visit seems, too, to remind a child that she made friends. She thinks, 'I may have left here, but I still have friends in this place.'"

Pepper suggests that preschool teachers begin to "play" kindergarten with the older children before they leave. This, too, will help the youngsters who are moving on get a sense of what regular school may be like.

A CHILD'S-EYE VIEW OF KINDERGARTEN

She's already had this adjustment, so it will be easy, a parent may think. And indeed the experience of preschool does, as we have said, make it somewhat easier for most children to adjust to kindergarten. Nevertheless, here is the way some kids may see it:

I don't know anyone.

There are so many children and they won't let my mom stay.

The teacher makes us be quiet.

I'm afraid of the big kids on the bus.

*In my other school I went in the morning. Here I have
to go all day.*

The work is too hard.

The bathroom is too far away.

I don't remember how to get to the room.

There is every evidence that children going to kindergarten may experience some anxiety and separation pangs,
even if they have been to preschool. Occasionally a child's
instinctive distrust of the new school is justified. Even in
the nicest kindergarten setting, children have a period of
adjustment. Parents should recognize this and help youngsters as much as possible.

A Last Word on Kindergarten

The most useful thing a parent can do is to preserve a good
preschool experience by making sure that kindergarten
will continue it. There is a distressing trend in some public
kindergartens to begin teaching the skills that used to be
the province of first grade. In this timetable, first grade
becomes second, second third, and so on. Parents need to
ask, ''Why? What's the rush?'' Kindergarten should be a
bridge year where children can make the transition comfortably and gradually from concrete to more abstract
modes of learning, instead of being rushed along to reach
their level of incompetence.

If you see a stultifying academic atmosphere surfacing
in your child's kindergarten class, you may want to talk
about it with the teacher, the school principal, and with
other parents. In a severe situation you may have to step
in and see to it that kindergarten does not undo all the
good that accrued in preschool. Here is another place

where the preschool director with whom you have a good relationship can continue to be helpful.

Closing the door on preschool signals the end of one stage of your child's education and the beginning of another. If you could imagine a smooth transition, it might go something like this:

▲ Your child has a chance to talk about kindergarten with his preschool teacher. She answers his questions and those of the other children.

• You and your youngster visit the school and spend some time in the classroom.

▪ You meet the kindergarten teacher. Perhaps she stops by at your house for a short visit.

▲ You talk with the principal (or director) about your child.

• You accompany your youngster to the classroom on the first day of school. When she comes home at the end of the first week she says, "I love kindergarten."

PRESCHOOL IN YOUR FUTURE

In the next ten years the number of young children who will be ready for developmentally appropriate preschool programs will increase by more than 50 percent. Just how that need will be met may in some measure determine the quality of life in America in the twenty-first century. If preschool can set the stage for learning, then who gets it and what kind it is is central to what kind of children we're going to raise. Unfortunately these upcoming population changes are occurring at a time when the country has a huge federal deficit. In the face of this staggering debt, many legislators seem unwilling to commit funds for an investment in our nation's children, in spite of the fact that countries poorer than we are (Canada, for instance) have subsidized child care at the preschool level. Whether this situation will change soon is in part up to parent voters.

If you expect to start a family or enlarge your present one, there are several preschool issues that you should keep an eye on, because they will directly affect you. You can perhaps help shape the ones you think are important to your family's life by getting involved in the community and/or keeping in touch with your legislators on the local, state, and federal level.

One thing to stay current on is the public pre-K movement (see page 22). Pre-K in the public schools, or financed by public and foundation partnerships, may well be the wave of the future for young parents having their first child now. But making sure that those programs are appropriate for young children is another story. Some educators are worried that once the public schools are in control, they'll move teachers around with little regard for whether an individual has the special training to teach young children. Others are concerned that pre-K will be turned into whole-day care, while their opponents worry that it won't. But even as educators fret, in some places they are solving these problems and getting the job done. The Franklin Early Childhood Center in Nassau County, New York, is a prime example of how you can achieve quality pre-K through a combined effort of public and private funding. This preschool center in public school District 14 provides quality developmentally appropriate education and care to children from ages three to five in a variety of programs tailored to the needs of parents. Here is some of what the district offers free of charge:

▲ Half-day pre-K for all four-year-olds in the district
• An extended day for four-year-olds whose parents choose it
▪ A classroom for three-year-olds who meet certain criteria
▲ A Parent Volunteer Training Center
• Being a Better Parent classes, for parents of children under two (in partnership with Nassau Medical Center—twenty dollars per term)
▪ A before-school program for preschoolers whose parents work
▲ A half-day kindergarten program for all eligible children, and an optional all-day kindergarten
• English-as-a-second-language classes for young children

All these activities take place in an underused elementary school that has been converted into a setting dedicated to preschoolers and their parents. It contains state-of-the-art equipment, early childhood teacher-created as well as standard materials, and a staff of certified teachers, district-trained assistant teachers, and parent volunteers, all dedicated to giving young children developmentally appropriate preschool.

One aspect of the center that is worth special mention is its relationship to later elementary school education. Parents often complain about the fact that their child gets a wonderful preschool education and then the elementary school doesn't measure up with comparable education. In the Hewlett-Woodmere School District, of which the Franklin Early Childhood Center is a part, the key word is *coordination*. Children's strengths and weaknesses are shared from grade to grade. In this and other respects,

Hewlett-Woodmere provides a model of what pre-K can be in the future.

But if every school district were to do this, who would foot the bill? The Committee for Economic Development has estimated that it would cost $3 billion a year to provide preschool programs just for all the poor four-year-olds in the country. But—say people who have studied the whole economic picture—poorly educated children cost us all, ultimately, in various social services. We could save about $10 billion in ultimate social service outlays if, for instance, Head Start were to serve all the eligible children.

Another question is the one of who will go to public preschool. Some educators favor a continued policy of concentrating on poor children and other children ''at risk.'' Others say that with the rise of both working parents and single-parent families, there is a growing demand for quality preschool education and care for all children. Should middle-class families pay for private preschool while poor children go free to public pre-K? To make middle-class families pay while poor kids go to public preschool is certainly a concept we all have to think hard about. Do we want our youngsters segregated from one another this way? Many educators believe that not only do all children learn from one another but that separations of this kind tend to widen an already widening social and economic gap.

No one knows as yet whether preschool education is going to be voluntary or mandatory, half-day or full-day, or whether it will be supplemented by afterschool care. Nor is it possible to foresee whether public pre-K is going to offer the entire answer to the preschool population explosion. In any case, parents need to get active in the schools, go to budget hearings, and keep in touch with how school policy is meeting the challenge of pre-K. It is invigorating how much you can do as far as school policy is concerned if you get in on the ground floor.

What seems to make the most sense is to look at preschool in other ways besides through the glass of public pre-K education. Public-private partnerships are possible, as are partnerships of business and government. In each of these ideas, the notion of adequate pay for early childhood teachers is a "given" and would help to ensure quality control. And what about an even stronger partnership with the parent for effective early education? One direction that is being tried experimentally is to allocate funds not for public preschool but directly to families so that they can stay home with their preschoolers instead of working. In this model, parents would get specific early childhood training so that their children would in a sense get an appropriate preschool education at home, beginning in infancy. This is not such a radical notion. Sweden, for example, subsidizes parental leave for nine months after a child is born, at 90 percent of salary. Mothers and fathers can share this time at home, and both therefore have a part in their youngster's earliest education.

WHAT HAPPENS BEFORE THREE

Perhaps the clearest case for parents as first teachers is the experimental program set up by educator Burton White. This project, called New Parents as Teachers (NPAT), was developed in conjunction with the Missouri State Department of Education and represents the first time that a public school system has become involved with the education of children from birth to three and has provided some kind of picture of the results.

White's program is based on training parents to be their child's first teachers. In fact, it points up the idea of the parenting partnership and even moves it down a few years.

The goal of the program was to teach parents how to make every child as "educated" as possible by the age of three. In fact, the results from the three hundred families involved seem to suggest that local public schools can help families guide their children toward the kinds of early learning we have been talking about here.

The tests of the NPAT children (all first-borns) showed that the children performed well on standard tests of mental processing and on school-related tests. Only 15 percent of school-age youngsters did better than the project three-year-olds. It is hard not to take these statistics seriously, particularly as they fit with what the program parents themselves saw.

Dr. White goes pretty far in his assessment of the importance of the preschool years. He believes that birth is the starting gate and that even preschool is too late to begin work on language and learning deficits. Parents may not want to buy that whole package, but if you are a new parent thinking about the future, such a program would give you a heightened sense of how important you are to your baby, because "Start early" is not only a message to be applied to looking for a specific preschool, it is also a specific in terms of your role in shaping your child's learning in the first three crucial years. If your child is going to be at home for the first three years, you certainly might want to look into the parenting program in your area, or start one, as part of the preparation for preschool.

KNOW YOUR ABC

In 1988 the U.S. Congress had before it a comprehensive child care bill. It is called "The Act for Better Child Care," or "ABC." It was introduced in November 1987 by Senator Christopher Dodd (Connecticut) and Representative Dale Kildee (Michigan). It provides $2.5 billion a year in funding for three years. The money will go toward improving child care, subsidizing care for working families on a sliding scale, cooperating with states to develop start-up preschool programs and referral services and to ensure a living wage for child care workers.

Although this bill failed to reach the floor for a final vote in the 1988 session of Congress, its supporters say ABC got a lot farther and moved a lot faster than most legislation in its first year of introduction. It is a good bill, and its advocates, including a coalition of 131 national organizations that form the Alliance for Better Child Care, are optimistic that they will do better in 1989.

ABC is only one of a number of pieces of legislation that you, as a parent, should know about. Also on the table is an alternate plan by the administration calling for additional tax credits for the families of preschool children. Under this plan poor families would get $1,000 credit for each child up to age four, whether or not the family pays for child care. Thus even parents who stay home would get aid; the plan is designed also to cover those families who can't claim the existing tax credit because their income is too low. Moreover, low-income families who owe no federal taxes could file for reimbursement for the amount they spend on child care, up to $1,000. Employers could pay the money in advance, in employee paychecks.

The Bush plan clearly is directed at low-income families. Marian Wright Edelman, president of the Children's Defense Fund, points out that with day care outside the home costing from $1,500 to $10,000 a year (the average being around $3,000), the administration's plan is at best only a modest family-income supplement.

Both of these proposals are likely to be modified during the coming year. If you want to keep informed, become active, and have your voice heard on matters related to child care, you can join the Child Care Action Campaign. Write to:

Child Care Action Campaign
99 Hudson Street
New York, New York 10013

A Final Word

No one can predict what is going to happen to preschool education in the next few years. But it's certainly safe to assume that the child born now will have a preschool experience significantly different from what his brother or sister is having today. However, the essentials of good preschool are not apt to change, nor will the need for a caring alliance among parent, school, and child. Both the venerable preschool idea and the preschool partnership are here to stay.

INDEX

ABOUT THE AUTHOR

Barbara Brenner has written more than fifty books for children, as well as numerous articles and books on subjects of interest to parents. She is the author of *Love and Discipline* and, with Joanne Oppenheim and Betty Boegehold, *Raising a Confident Child* and *Choosing Books for Kids*. She has taught and conducted workshops for teachers at Bank Street College, has taught writing at Parsons School of Design, and has lectured to parents, teachers, and librarians all over the country on subjects related to children's writing and reading.

The Brenners have two grown sons and live in Pennsylvania.

ABOUT BANK STREET COLLEGE

The Bank Street School for Children is a laboratory school for Bank Street College of Education and a working model of the College's approach to learning and teaching. The school offers a rich learning environment for 450 children from the ages of three to thirteen, and it provides the College with a setting for teacher training, research, and the development of curriculum materials. This collaborative effort between the College staff and school faculty focuses on the *developmental-interaction* approach to learning.

Developmental refers to the patterns discernible as children grow physically, mentally, emotionally, and socially. *Interaction* includes not only the child's relationship with his or her physical environment, and with other children and adults, but also the internal interactions between the intellect and the emotions.

This approach can be applied in home life just as well as in school life. For of all the child's teachers the first and most enduring ones are the parents. Bank Street's philosophy concretely supports parents and other caregivers by helping children explore and better understand their world; by sharing interests and ideas with children while allowing them to develop their own curiosity; and by establishing a value system as a framework for and a guide to children's growing independence.

This approach to learning puts great emphasis on child development and individual learning styles, the importance of experiential learning, and the understanding that the emotional life of children is inseparable from their learning, interests, and motivation.

It is perhaps a misnomer to call the Bank Street approach experimental or nontraditional. For more than sixty years Bank Street has influenced educational theory and practice in both private and public schools. It has trained teachers, administrators, and other children's advocates, who in turn have played a vital role in shaping policies and practice in schools, museums, hospitals, and child care settings. Unlike some private schools, at Bank Street the students are not all drawn from middle- and upper-class families. Thirty-five percent of the children attend the School for Children on full or partial scholarship. Furthermore, through its Follow-Through program, the Bank Street model has been carried to schools in the inner cities and rural settings all over the United States.

Bank Street has always considered the best teaching/ learning situation to include three partners—teacher, parent, and child.